SACRAMENT MOST HOLY

SACRAMENT MOST HOLY

RONALD KNOX

CLUNY
Providence, Rhode Island

CLUNY EDITION, 2025

For more information regarding this title
or any other Cluny publication,
please write to info@clunymedia.com, or to
Cluny Media, P.O. Box 1664, Providence, RI 02901
WWW.CLUNYMEDIA.COM

These sermons originally appeared in *Heaven and Charing Cross* (1935), *The Window in the Wall* (1956), and *Pastoral Sermons* (1960). The text of this volume follows that given by Fr. Philip Caraman, S.J., in *Pastoral Sermons and* retains his editorial references and revisions.

Heaven and Charing Cross copyright © 1935, *The Window in the Wall* copyright © 1956, and *Pastoral Sermons* copyright © 1960, by Lady Magdalen Howard

Published by permission. All rights reserved

NIHIL OBSTAT:
D. Smith, S.Th.D., Ph.D., *Censor deputatus*
Hubertus Richards, S.T.D., L.S.S., *censor deputatus*

IMPRIMATUR: Joseph Butt, *Vicar capitular*
WESTMONASTERII, DIE 6 FEBRUARII, 1935

E. Morrogh Bernard, *vicarius generalis*
WESTMONASTERI: DIE 10 JANUARII 1960

Cluny edition copyright © 2024 Cluny Media LLC

ISBN (PAPERBACK): 978-1685953775

Cover design by Clarke & Clarke
Cover image: Luca Signorelli,
Communion of the Apostles,
oil on panel, c. 1512
Courtesy of Wikimedia Commons

CONTENTS

I.	The Window in the Wall	1
II.	The City of Peace	8
III.	Hired Servants	15
IV.	Where God Lives	22
V.	Giving of Thanks	30
VI.	As Your Servant	38
VII.	The Gleaner	44
VIII.	Peace in Ourselves	52
IX.	The Mass and the Ritual	58
X.	The Best Man	65
XI.	Self-Examination	72
XII.	The Thing That Matters	80
XIII.	Real Bread	87
XIV.	This Mass and the Mass	94
XV.	The Pattern of His Death	101
XVI.	The Challenge	108
XVII.	A Better Country	114
XVIII.	Jesus My Friend	121
XIX.	First and Last Communions	128
XX.	Pity for the Multitude	135
XXI.	One Body	141
XXII.	Bread and Wine	149

XXIII.	*Prope est Verbum*	157
XXIV.	*Novum Pascha Novae Legis*	165
XXV.	*The Great Supper*	172
XXVI.	*A Priest for Ever*	179
XXVII.	*Words of Life*	188
XXVIII.	*The Hidden God*	196
XXIX.	*The Mirror of Conscience*	203
XXX.	*Bread from Heaven*	211
XXXI.	*The Divine Sacrifice*	218

I

The Window in the Wall

And now he is standing on the other side of this very wall; now he is looking through each window in turn, peering through every chink. I can hear my true love calling to me, Rise up, rise up quickly, dear heart, so gentle, so beautiful, rise up and come with me. (CANT. 2:9)

SET IN THE MIDDLE of the Old Testament, in striking contrast to those collections of dry aphorisms which come before and after it, the Canticle of Canticles occupies a position unique in sacred literature. In form it is a drama, in literary inspiration it is a love poem, such as might have graced any anthology in any language; it has, in its literal acceptation, no connection with theology from beginning to end. It is the story, apparently, of a young bride carried away to the harem of King Solomon, yet true to her lover, who comes and calls to her, rescues her from her gilded bondage, and takes her back to freedom and to her country home. And that book, as we all know, is a kind of palimpsest, in which the saints of every age have read between the lines, and found there the appropriate language in which to express their love for God, God's love for them. No part of the Old Testament gives rise more easily to outraged astonishment, to pharisaical scandal, when it comes into the hands of the profane: that *this* should be reckoned as sacred literature! No part of the

RONALD KNOX

Old Testament, I suppose, has more endeared itself to the greatest friends of Christ; they would have spared all the rest to save this. In the passage from which I have taken my text, the voice of the country lover makes itself heard, all of a sudden, amid the distractions of Solomon's court. He stands close to the wall of the harem, and whispers through the window. The voice of the beloved—everywhere, in the mystical interpretation of the poem, the voice of the beloved is understood of Christ speaking to the faithful soul. And that voice at the window brings to my own mind a fancy which I have often had, which I suppose many of us have had before now, in looking at the sacred Host enthroned in the monstrance. The fancy, I mean, that the glittering disc of whiteness which we see occupying that round opening is not reflecting the light of the candles in front of it, but is penetrated with a light of its own, a light not of this world, shining through it from behind, as if through a window, outdazzling gold and candle-flame with a more intense radiance. Such a visual impression you may have just for a moment, then you reflect that it is only an illusion; and then on further thought you question, Is it an illusion? Is it not rather the truth, but a truth hidden from our eyes, that the Host in the monstrance, or rather those accidents of it which make themselves known to our senses, are a kind of window through which a heavenly light streams into our world; a window giving access on a spiritual world outside our human experience?

Behold, he stands behind "our wall"; the wall of our corrupt nature, which shuts us off from breathing, as man breathed in the days of his innocency, the airs of heaven; the wall of sense, which cheats us when we try even to imagine eternity; the wall of immortified affection, which shuts us in with creatures and allows

Sacrament Most Holy

them to dominate our desires; the wall of pride, which makes us feel, except when death or tragedy is very close to us, so independent and self-sufficient. Our wall—we raised it against God, not he against us; we raised it, when Adam sinned, and when each of us took up again, by deliberate choice, that legacy of sinfulness in his own life. And through that wall the Incarnation and the Passion of Jesus Christ have made a great window; St Paul tells us so; "he made both one, breaking down the wall that was a barrier between us" (Eph. 2:14), as the temple veil was torn in two on the day when he suffered. He "made both one"; made our world of sin and sight and sense one with the spiritual world; made a breach in our citadel, let light into our prison.

Not for a moment, amid the confusion of an historical situation; the window is there for all time, if we would only recognize it. He himself, in his risen and glorified body, is the window between the two worlds. As the window belongs both to the room inside and to the open air outside, so his glorified body belongs at once to time and to eternity; belongs to time, because he took it upon himself, when he was born in time of his blessed Mother, belongs to eternity, because it is now transfigured with the light of glory which is part of our future inheritance. That glory is something human eyes cannot bear to see; when Moses had talked with God on Mount Sinai, he came back with his face shining, so that he had to put a veil over it lest the people's eyes should dazzle when they beheld him; and if he, who was only God's ambassador, who had only spoken with God in the darkness, was so illuminated by it, what of him who is himself God, whose human nature has been caught up into the Abyss of all being? When he rose from the dead, and

RONALD KNOX

still for forty days walked about our earth, that glory was hidden from mortal eyes by a special dispensation. And now, now that he reigns in heaven, he will make himself manifest on earth still; but his glory will be veiled, more jealously than ever, as he confronts, now, the gaze of the sinner and the doubter, as he gives himself into the hands of the unworthy.

We all know what veil it is that covers him now; it is the mystery which occupies our thoughts this morning. In this mystery of transubstantiation, he has broken into the very heart of nature, and has separated from one another in reality two elements which we find it difficult to separate even in thought, the inner substance of things from those outward manifestations of it which make it known to our senses. Burn all the candles you will in front of it, call to your aid all the resources of science, and flood it with a light stronger than human eyes can bear to look upon, still that white disc will be nothing better than a dark veil, hiding the ineffable light of glory which shines in and through the substance of Christ's ascended body. A veil, that is what we look at, a curtain drawn over the window, as you may curtain the windows of a sick-room, because the patient's eyes are not strong enough to face the full glare of daylight. But behind that curtain, all the time, is the window which lets our world communicate with the world of the supernatural. As the angels ascended and descended on Jacob's ladder, so here our prayers go out into the unseen, so here grace comes flooding through, like a rushing mighty wind, into the stagnant air of our earthly experience.

And at the window, behind the wall of partition that is a wall of partition no longer, stands the Beloved himself, calling us out into

Sacrament Most Holy

the open; calling us away from the ointments and the spikenard of Solomon's court, that stupefy and enchain our senses, to the gardens and the vineyards, to the fields and the villages, to the pure airs of eternity. Arise (he says), make haste and come. Come away from the blind pursuit of creatures, from all the plans your busy brain evolves for your present and future pleasures, from the frivolous distractions it clings to. Come away from the pettiness and the meanness of your everyday life, from the grudges, the jealousies, the unhealed enmities that set your imagination throbbing. Come away from the cares and solicitudes about the morrow that seem so urgent, your heavy anxieties about the world's future and your own, so short either of them and so uncertain. Come away into the wilderness of prayer, where my love will follow you and my hand hold you; learn to live, with the innermost part of your soul, with all your secret aspirations, with all the centre of your hopes and cares, in that supernatural world which can be yours now, which must be yours hereafter.

Not that he calls us, yet, away from the body, from its claims and its necessities; that call will come in his own time. Nor yet that the occupations, and the amusements of this life, his creatures, given us for our use, are to be despised and set aside as something evil. Rather, as a beam of sunlight coming through the window lights up and makes visible the tiny motes of dust that fill the air, so those who live closest to him find, in the creatures round about them, a fresh charm and a fresh meaning, which the jaded palate of worldliness was too dull to detect. But he wants our hearts; *ut inter mundanas varietates ibi fixa sint corda ubi vera sunt gaudia*—our hearts must be there fixed, where are pure joys, before we can begin to see earth in its right perspective. We must be weaned away from earth first; and the means by which he does that is holy communion. That is the medicine which enables the enfeebled soul to look steadily at the divine light, to breathe deeply of the unfamiliar air. I wonder, is that why some of us are so frightened of holy communion, because we still cling so to the world of sense? It is certain that Catholics are most apt to neglect communion just when they most need it; in the spring-time of youth, when the blood is hot, and the passions strong, and ambition dominates us. Why is that, unless that we are more wedded, when we are young, to the desires that perish? I wonder, is that why so many of us who go often to communion find that it makes, apparently, little difference to us; that we are still as full of bad habits as we were ten or fifteen years ago, that our lives, if anything, compare unfavourably with the lives of others, who have not our opportunities for going to communion frequently? Is it perhaps because, all the time, we are shrinking from the act of confidence which would throw the whole burden of our lives on our Lord; we do not want holy communion to have its proper effect on us, which is to make the joys and distractions of this world have less meaning and less appeal for us? We must not expect him to work the marvels of his grace in us, if we oppose its action through the stubbornness of our own wills, still clinging to self and to sense.

Meanwhile, it is certain that as life goes on he reminds us, more and more, how transitory it is and how unsatisfactory, by taking from us the supports which allowed our hearts to rest in this world. Our friends are taken from us by death; and if we would reach them now we must pierce beyond the veil; must live in Christ if we are

Sacrament Most Holy

to be one, consciously, with those who sleep in him. May God have mercy on their souls, and grant them light in their place of waiting; and may he grant us, who have adored him today beneath the veil of his sacramental presence, grace to hear his voice, and obey his call, and live with him in heavenly places, until he calls us, too, to himself, and makes us glad at last with the beauty of his unveiled presence.

II

The City of Peace

Jerusalem is built like a city which is one in fellowship. (Ps. 121:3)

A CITY which is one in fellowship—a city isolated by its position from the rest of the world, and therefore dependent for its very existence on the mutual good-will of its inhabitants. Palestine lies, as we know—we were never more conscious of it than today—across one of the great strategic highways of the world. It is on the direct route between Egypt and Northern Asia; and its plain of Megiddo was consequently a place where the armies of opposing empires were always meeting in conflict. We shall hear of it again, for it is the valley of Armageddon. But Jerusalem itself stands remote among the hills, as if to let the rumours of world-history pass it by. Let Samaria enjoy the rich cultivation of the plains, and feel every passing tide of conflict between North and South; Jerusalem, safe on its lonely peaks, was to look down on this pageant of history undisturbed. The world was to sweep round its feet, leaving it alone and unconquered through the centuries. Meanwhile, its inhabitants, so cut off from commerce with their kind, were to be bound together by strong ties of civic unity; it was to be the city of

---

This sermon was preached early in the Second World War.

Sacrament Most Holy

peace, its very name announced that. A grand destiny, partly but imperfectly fulfilled.

Is it fanciful of us to detect in this providential accident of sacred geography, a type, a symbol, of that institution which, more than anything else, represents and secures for us Christian people the supernatural unity by which and in which we live; I mean, the institution of the Holy Eucharist? The Christian altar, like the temple at Jerusalem, is the rallying-point of God's people. Here, as there, heaven touches earth, yet remains uncontaminated by its contact. Christ is not moved when the sacrament is moved, is not broken when the sacrament is broken; so close does he come to our experience of daily life, so remote does he remain from it. And one of the chief influences he exerts, one of the chief ends he attains, by that nearness of his, is to draw us, his children, closer together. It is the sacrament of peace, as Jerusalem was the city of peace; through it we are one in fellowship. We speak of Christians as united in a single communion, of one Christian body as being in communion with, or out of communion with, another; that is no accident, no abuse of language. The whole notion of Christian solidarity grows out of, and is centred in, the common participation of a common table. As the many grains of wheat are ground together into one loaf, as the many grapes are pressed together in one cup, so we, being many, are one in Christ. How could we be one with Christ, without becoming one in Christ? I could quote a hundred phrases from the liturgy which insist on this doctrine, now so little remembered, or at least so much disregarded. But it will be sufficient to refer you to the liturgy of today's feast, the Corpus Christi feast. Look at the secret prayer which the priest will be saying in your name a few minutes

RONALD KNOX

from now; what does it say? "Grant, Lord, to thy Church the gifts of unity and peace, which are mystically betokened by these gifts we are offering to thee."[1] Unity and peace—even the unconsecrated elements, the Church tells us, are meant to be symbolical of that.

Under the old dispensation, you see, the yearly sacrifice of the Passover was the signal for the reunion of all faithful Jews at a common centre. "His parents went up every year to Jerusalem"—every year, our Lady and St Joseph had the opportunity of meeting Zachary and Elizabeth; they had no difficulty in keeping alive the gracious bond of family affection. So it was with all the pious Jews of their time; it was like the diocesan pilgrimage to Lourdes on a grand scale. When the new covenant superseded the old, it was the daily sacrifice of the Mass, instead of the yearly sacrifice of the Passover, that became the rallying-point of God's people. The primitive Church in Jerusalem broke bread from day to day from house to house; visibly and consciously they were a single family. And when the Gospel spread to different centres all over the Mediterranean world, each local church prepared itself for the celebration of the divine mysteries with an *agape*, a love-feast, at which rich and poor sat down together; you may read in the first epistle to the Corinthians how deeply distressed St Paul was by any behaviour on the part of Christians which threatened to obscure the significance of that common act. And although the Church, scattered over three continents, could no longer muster all her membership within four walls, it was felt from the first that every Christian was mystically united to all other Christians by his participation in the mysteries.

---

1. Secret Prayer for the feast of Corpus Christi.

Sacrament Most Holy

That is why St Ignatius, early in the second century, speaks of the Roman Church as presiding over the *agape,* the communion of all faithful Christians everywhere. That is why each local church would write up, on tablets over the altar, the names of neighbouring bishops, so as to be one with them in prayer. The Church throughout the world was the new people of God, and its Jerusalem, its stronghold of peace, was not any local centre; it was in a common meal that they found themselves mystically united to one another.

That supernatural unity is still laid up for us, if we would only realize it, in the tabernacle. Christian people, however much separated by long distances of land or sea, meet together in full force, by a mystical reunion, whenever and wherever the bread is broken, and the cup blessed. We do well to remember that notion in times like these. War is a sword; it brings division into our lives. It severs nation from nation; at the moment we have less opportunity of exchanging ideas with our fellow Catholics on the continent of Europe than at any time within living memory. But when we communicate, you and I, we sit at a common table with them, we are united, even with our enemies, by a bond of mystical fellowship. Families, everywhere, are being split up; here, young men and women have been called away to distant centres in the service of their country; there, children have been separated from their parents, to ensure their safety in times of peril. Increasing difficulty of communication, whether across the seas or within our own island, is underlining the difficulty; how seldom, comparatively, can we meet old friends now, how difficult it is to arrange a reunion of families at Christmas time, or of friends for social enjoyment! A sense of isolation is creeping over us, of old ties broken and old associations forgotten; we cling to everything that will unite us to one another. And shall we not cling, above all, to the sacrament which provides us with a real opportunity of making ourselves one with those we love? Bitterest of all, at such times, death comes close to us and breaks up our circles of family and of friendship; but death itself cannot dissever the bond of Christian unity which joins us to our dead. We remember God's servants and handmaids who have gone before us, outstripped us in the race for eternity; who now sleep in the sleep of peace, while we must watch still in the watchfulness of war. And remembering them, we are still one with them; not by sentimental make-believe, but in a real fellowship, closer and more enduring, could we but realize it, than all the bonds of earth.

On that altar, Christ is present; is present in space, though not under the conditions of space. And wherever the words of consecration are pronounced, a hundred miles from here, a thousand miles from here, Christ is present in the same way. Is that a different Christ? No, the same Christ, present here and equally present a thousand miles away. Is it possible to doubt that we are near to those we love, when we and they are equally near to Christ, equally present to both of us? And if that is true, even when we kneel before the tabernacle, does it not become more startlingly, more significantly true when we and they partake together, whatever leagues of distance intervene, of this body and blood, given to us in holy communion? Equally united to the same Christ, are not we and they united together, more closely in fact than if we could see one another's faces, hear one another's voices, sitting in the same room? And did we complain that we are *separated* from those we love? It is our fault or theirs if we are.

Sacrament Most Holy

War has sundered the nations—yes, it can interrupt the exchange of commerce, of ideas, of diplomatic courtesies. It cannot interrupt the current of sacramental fellowship which unites us with all Christians, even with our enemies, when we and they partake of the same heavenly banquet. Only an unworthy reception, on their side or on ours, can interrupt that. The bread and wine which the priest will be offering a moment from now are gifts of unity and of peace, making us one with all our fellow Catholics, in Poland, in France, yes, in Italy and Germany too. Years may have to elapse before the external conditions of free intercourse are re-established between us. But by the greatest of all titles, as children round our Father's table, we are already at one. The Blessed Sacrament, the Jerusalem of our souls, stands apart from and above all the ebb and flow of world-politics, its citizenship a common fellowship between us and those who are estranged from us, those who at the moment are our enemies. Our friends yesterday, our friends tomorrow—in the timeless existence to which that altar introduces us, they are our friends today.

War has divided families, and circles of familiar acquaintance—yes, it can interpose distance between us and those we love, make it difficult, sometimes, to obtain news of them, to exchange our good offices with theirs. It cannot interpose a barrier between us and them, so long as both draw near to the source of all real unity, the heart of Jesus Christ. In the hour when this sacrament was first instituted, not all the apostles were equally close to their Master in space; only to St John was it given to rest his head on his Friend's bosom. But all alike were united to their Master and to one another—all except one, separated from his Master, separated from his fellow apostles, by the estranging influence of unrepented sin. In absence from our homes, in perilous places, in prison it may be, or in exile, we are still united, all of us, unless that same barrier should intervene.

War divides men's souls from their bodies; and in doing so, divides us, irreparably, it seems, from those we love. And, this time, we can no longer console ourselves with the reflection that we and they, in spite of distance, can meet at one altar and share one meal. For them, the use of sacramental means has come to an end, with the body itself, and whatever grace visits them now must clothe itself in other forms than those to which we are accustomed. And yet the Church clings, obstinately, to the instinct which tells her that they, too, are somehow partakers of the altar; no Mass is complete unless they, too, are remembered. An empty place at table, yes, and an empty chair by the fireside, but not an empty place at the communion rail—that sacrament which unites the living unites too, somehow, the living with the dead. Union with Christ is given to each of us in accordance with the needs of his state. To us, living men who live by bread, he comes under the form of bread; to those others, who belong to a world of spirits, he must impart himself in other ways. He makes them one with himself, none the less surely for that; it is only our imaginations that are at fault if we find it difficult to remember that they, too, are with us; if we could see things with their eyes, should we not find them, perhaps, closer than ever to our side? Neither life nor death nor any other creature can separate us from the love of Christ; in that love, we are all one; without it, we should be crying to one another helplessly in the dark. May he draw us all nearer together by drawing us, continually, nearer to himself.

III

Hired Servants

How many hired servants there are in my father's house, who have more bread than they can eat, and here am I perishing with hunger.

(LUKE 15:17)

WE ALL KNOW the parable of the prodigal son nearly by heart; we can all see for ourselves how accurately it delineates the experiences of the penitent sinner; many of us find it linked, by a sad chain of memories, to the history of our own lives. You see him, the prodigal, receiving a patrimony from his father without gratitude, taking it as a matter of course; and you consider how little we value, commonly, our patrimony of divine grace until we come to lose it. You see him starting off for a far country, just turning to wave farewell at the end of the drive, as he slaps the new cheque-book in his pocket; and you consider how lightly, how carelessly we Christians will march off into the midst of spiritual dangers. You see him wasting his money in riotous living, and caught unawares by the great famine for which he had made no provision; you consider how we men waste our capital of grace through neglect, until at last the occasion of sin finds us out, and we fall without a struggle. You see him sunk in the pig-sty's degradation, and then visited by a gracious touch of home-sickness; rousing himself

RONALD KNOX

suddenly, and squaring his shoulders for the humiliating journey to his father's house; you consider how grace uses our human instability of mind to make us grow weary of our sins, drives us back to God, who is our heart's rest. You see the father running out to meet the prodigal, forgiving him, restoring him to favour, making a feast in his honour; you consider how God loves to forgive, how prompt is his pardon, and how full, and how effective; how in absolution that which was dead comes to life again, that which was lost is found.

All *that* we remember, the main structure of the story; I am not sure that we always give sufficient attention to the details, the exquisite touches with which this epic of the human heart is etched in. Here is one, apparently very unimportant, which will give us enough material for a whole sermon this morning, and dispose us for the better celebration of today's feast. What was the train of thought which produced, at last, repentance in the prodigal? What was the loophole by which grace shone into the prison of his soul? He is in the fields, feeding swine; anybody who has done that, knows how the spectacle absorbs the onlooker—this hurrying, jostling pageant of animal life has something of the grandeur of a waterfall; the whole world seems to be full of eating, as you watch. It does not take any long stretch of the imagination for the poor prodigal to be brought to a sense of his own condition, half-starved in this strange country where only man goes wanting, and the beasts have their fill. Those husks we read of were used, are still used, for human food. But the bucket has been overturned now; there will be no crumbs left for the prodigal. So hungry; he has never known before what it was to work for hire.

Sacrament Most Holy

For hire—and yet, to be a paid workman is not always to be underpaid. He thinks of the men who used to work on his father's estate; as a little boy he used to watch them, fascinated, when they sat down under a hedge and undid those mysterious pudding-basins, tied up in coloured handkerchiefs, they carried their meals in. *They* never seemed to be hungry; there was no hoarding scraps about *them*; he can remember picking up some of the bread they had left lying about and feeding the ducks with it. So his mind runs on; associations of memory assert themselves easily in a brain weakened by want of food. Are they still at work, he wonders, laying that piece of road, mending that hedge? And then suddenly, the contrast forces itself upon his mind; "How many hired servants of my father have more bread than they want, and here am I, dying of hunger!" Here, among strangers; here, miserably employed; here, when there was never any need for me to have left my home. "I will arise, and will go to my father, and say to him, Father, I have sinned." One train of thought has led from the swill-tub to the prodigal's return.

So much for the parable; and now, what of the interpretation of the parable? What is this hunger for food which only becomes articulate at the sight of beasts feeding, and then expresses itself in a hunger for home? It is the hunger of the immortal soul for God; he has made us for himself, and our hearts cannot rest until they find rest in him. The soul that has plunged into vicious habits, and seems so deeply sunk in them, now, that there is no chance of a recovery, still finds itself dissatisfied with the brief enjoyments, the narrow horizons, of earth. It looks round it at the pig-sty that has become its world; conceives a distaste and a contempt for the sinners who share that world, no better than a herd of swine, foot in trough, grunting and scrambling; was man born for this? And then, on a rebound, the half-repentant mind turns away from the beast-world that surrounds it to the angel-world from which it came out, and which must for ever be its goal; "How many of my father's servants..."—was not that service, after all, perfect freedom? "And I, here, perish with hunger"; here, far from the thought of God, here, environed with corruption; here, where nothing but my own pride and obstinacy stands between me and my home. "I will arise, and go to my father, and say, I have sinned."

With us Catholics, brought up to the life of the sacraments, this longing for God makes itself felt more, expresses itself best, in hunger for our souls' bread, the Holy Eucharist. This supernatural food has become, as it were, our natural food; without it we languish. Oh, we may be rare communicants, we may be indevout communicants, and not feel the loss; but once we cut ourselves off from it altogether, the hunger is there; faint, perhaps, perilously faint, but unmistakable. God knows how many souls there are all round us who are living, year after year, a maimed life; smothering, all the time, a secret bitterness that gnaws at the heart—because they have drifted away from their communions, and know that they cannot really do without them. With some of them, sin has turned into an inveterate habit; they shrink from the confessional, because they no longer feel that they have the power to shake it off. Some have married without the sanction of the Church, and are deprived of the sacraments while they persist in an attitude of rebellion. With some, faith itself has grown numb; they say they do not believe the doctrine of the Holy Eucharist is true, and yet, not believing it true, they wish it were true, so that they might go back to their starting-point, regain the home and the table they have lost.

Now, when the touch of grace comes, effectively, to those souls, as God grant it may, they will be in the prodigal's position. They will turn aside disgustedly from the flat and shallow consolations of the world they live in; they will remember the ease, and the contentment, and the confidence of living in their Father's home; and their eyes will turn enviously towards what, towards whom? Towards you and me.

God forgive us, towards you and me. "How many hired servants of my father"—we are those hired servants; privileged with a privilege they only can estimate who stand far off and perish with hunger. The hired servants have more bread than they can eat, more bread than they know what to do with. It is the word used of those fragments that were taken up after the feeding of the five thousand. Your communions and mine, what are they like? What sense do they show of the privilege we enjoy, of the possibilities that are open to us? How casual is the preparation that earns them for us, the thanksgiving that crowns them for us! How ready we are to forgo them, on some slight excuse of health or work; how little they mean to us, an hour after they have happened! Should not we do well, perhaps, to take the prodigal's words on our lips, but to read them the other way round? "How many sons there are, sons of my Father, outside their Father's house, perishing with hunger; and I here have more than I can eat, have more of *sacramental* grace offered me than I know what to do with!"

Hired servants of my father—is it, perhaps, because we are *hired* servants of God that we make so little of our opportunities? These others, who have rebelled against him, betrayed by passion, who have fallen away from him, discouraged by human weakness—how often they are really sons, though sons in exile! How often there is a generosity about their failings, which is lacking to our virtues! If they come back to him, when they come back to him, they will be the Magdalens, the Augustines, the great penitents, and therefore the great Christians. What a tragedy that they, who might serve him so well, have wandered away from him; that we, who have stayed at home like the stay-at-home elder brother, should be so second-rate!

We act like hired servants, if we take pains to do no more for God than bare duty demands of us, jealously watching, as it were, the terms of our contract with him. The priest gets up and goes back to the sacristy, and we are on our feet before he can reach the door. We act like hired servants, if we think of our communions only as they affect ourselves. "I go once a month," you say, "and really I don't seem to need more than that; there is very little to mention, as a rule, when confession-time comes round." Is that all the body and blood of Christ means to you, a kind of talisman to keep down the number of your sins? Or you say, "I'm not unhappy about my communions; because when I make them and just after I've made them I always have such a wonderful sense of peace, of consolation." Is that all the body and blood of Christ means to you, a kind of spiritual treat you can indulge in now and again? When we go to communion, you and I, we should aim at nothing less than making the life of Jesus Christ ours; immolating ourselves to God, annihilating ourselves before God, in him and through him and in union with his sacrifice, so that we can say, "It is no longer

Sacrament Most Holy

I that live; it is Christ lives in me" (Gal. 2:20). Until we aim at that, the bread of our Master's house is being wasted on us; we are hired servants, asking, and receiving, nothing better than a pittance for our livelihood.

Oh, if we could only realize that the Holy Eucharist is *panis fortium*, the bread of the strong! That it is meant to energize us and vitalize us, not merely to discipline and to soothe us! Let us pray our blessed Lady and all the saints of the Blessed Sacrament to win for us, in these times that are so difficult, and that are going to be so difficult, so dark for the future of religion, more generosity in our dealings with God, more boldness and imaginativeness in the graces we ask from him. "Father, give me the portion of the inheritance that falls to me"—are we justified in thinking of that as an impudent request? Or was the prodigal right in asking for his patrimony, and only wrong in the use he made of it? The elder son, who asked for nothing, gave nothing, did nothing.... May the grace of this holy feast be new life, new energy, new adventurousness to us all.

IV

Where God Lives

Daily I must listen to the taunt, Where is thy God now? (Ps. 41:4)

Tell me, my true love, where is now thy pasture-ground, where now is thy resting-place under the noon's heat? (Cant. 1:6)

They said to him, Where dost thou live? He said to them, Come and see; so they went and saw where he lived, and they stayed with him all the rest of the day, from about the tenth hour onwards. (John 1:38)

IF IT MAY BE SAID WITH REVERENCE, what a bad story-teller is St John! His gospel is a series of fragments—infinitely precious fragments, but fragments nevertheless—preserved from the hoarded memories of a very old man, who follows his own train of thought, as old men will, not stopping to consider what details it is that his hearers want to know. Nobody, you might say, would have been a worse journalist. He just recalls for us those unforgettable hours when he and St Andrew paid an afternoon call on our blessed Lord in his own lodging-place, and put the sun to rest as they sat talking with him. On that memory his mind reposes, and he tells us no more—what manner of habitation it was, whether our Lord was staying with friends, or with his Mother, or quite alone, what his

Sacrament Most Holy

habits of life were, all the things we want to know. Our Lord lodged with Zacchaeus, he lodged with Martha and Mary; otherwise the gospels tell us little about the entertainment earth gave to Jesus of Nazareth, the man who had nowhere to lay his head. For once, we think we are to hear more, and we go away disappointed.

And yet St John himself had felt just that curiosity, long before. What a natural instinct it is, when we meet somebody casually whose personality impresses itself on us, dominates us, to want to see more of him, and to want to see him in his own setting, against his own background, where he lives! The pictures on the walls, the books that lie on the shelves, the very knick-knacks on the mantelpiece will have something, surely, to tell us about him; they will make a frame for his personality, and we shall feel that we know him better. So it is with the bride in the Canticles—in those voluptuous airs of King Solomon's harem, her lover is out of place, he does not fit into the picture; let her see him among his flocks in the still, midday countryside, and she will know him as he is. So it was with St John and St Andrew; they know our Lord only as passer-by in the crowded ways; they follow as if to track him down to his lodging, and he divines their purpose, and invites them to pass the rest of the day there. What kind of picture are we to form of it? Possible, no doubt, that when Nicodemus came to see our Lord by night he found him in some rich dwelling where a devout host made everything comfortable for him. But I think we are more inclined to imagine the scene of that sacred hospitality as a more makeshift affair; a deserted house, perhaps, with the windows half boarded up; a straw mattress in a corner and not much else in the way of furniture; or just a cave in the cliffs, beyond Jordan. And this is the Prince who has come to suffer for his people; this is the palace which suffices for his earthly needs! Such was the kind of picture, I imagine, that conjured itself up in the memory of the old apostle, and he did not tell us about it; why should he? After all, it is what we should expect.

At the same time, I think St John will have read in that old question of his, "Master, where dost thou live?" the echo of a much older question which has been tormenting humanity since man's eyes were first troubled with a human soul. King David complains of those enemies who mocked at his misfortunes by asking him, "Where is thy God?" And we, because the age in which we live is impatient of old formulas, because the set of its mind is against the supernatural, share, often enough, that confusion and hesitation of his. "Where is your God?" they ask us. "Men of science have swept the heavens with their telescopes, and they have not found him. They have peered with their microscopes into the very heart of being, and they have brought us no word of him. Does he dwell in infinite space? But we are not sure, any longer, that space itself is infinite. Where is he, that we may worship him? Where is he, that we may reproach him for all the unhappiness that he allows to mar his creation?" These questions of theirs, though it be only at the back of our minds, disconcert us; we know that they are foolish, based on a wrong apprehension of what it is that spirit means, and how it is related to matter. But for all that the imagination, tied down as it is to the world of space and of sense, will not be satisfied by the answers which commend themselves to the reason. We demand that, somehow, we should be allowed to locate the presence of God as concentrated and focused in one particular spot. "Master," we cry,

Sacrament Most Holy

"*where* dost thou live?" We know, of course, that he is everywhere, that he cannot be confined in space, we still we ask for evidences of his presence, and would trace the influence of it, if we might, *here* rather than *here*. When a storm of wind howls about our ears with unaccustomed fury, we catch an echo, as it were, of his omnipotence; when a sunset paints the sky with unwonted richness of colour, it seems like a mirror, however imperfect, of his uncreated beauty. But the illusion only lasts for a moment; when we think about it, we realize that this is a trick of the fancy; we are isolating an experience and making something divine of it; God is not in fact any nearer to us—how could he be nearer to us?—in the storm than in calm, in the cool of evening than under the brazen sky of noon. God is everywhere, but he is not here or there, that we should find him here or there more than anywhere else.

Has he done nothing, then, to make it easier for us to find him? Why yes, surely; in the mystery of his Incarnation, so full of his condescension, this is perhaps the greatest condescension of all—that he who is without limit should be limited, as Incarnate, to one position in space. When Moses drew near to the burning bush, when Elias heard from his cave a whisper of the divine voice, God manifested his presence in a special way, but that was all. When our Lady bent over the crib at Bethlehem, God was *there*. It was not necessary for her to say, "Where is thy pasture ground, where now is thy resting-place?"—he lay in her arms, he fed at her breast. It was no use for the scornful unbeliever to challenge St John or St Andrew with the old question, "Where is thy God?"—those first apostles could say, and did say, "Come and see." For thirty-three years of human history it was possible to say, "There is God! Look, where

25

he feeds, with publicans and sinners! Look, where he lies, asleep in the forepart of a ship which the waves threaten with destruction!"

Yes, for thirty-three years: but afterwards? We can make our pilgrimage to the holy places, pass along the roads which were once trodden by divine feet, mount the hill on which our Lord suffered, worship, perhaps, at his very tomb. But it is all a story of yesterday; what use is it (we complain) that God should draw near to us in space, if he does not also draw near to us in time? It is not enough that *our* God should make himself present to *us*; why does not *my* God make himself present to *me*?

As we know, God has foreseen that complaint of ours, and has condescended to make provision for it. Everything else about the Blessed Sacrament may be obscure to us; we do not see our Lord as he is, we cannot fathom the mystery of that change which is effected in the consecrated elements, we have no clue to the manner in which holy communion imparts its virtue to our souls. But one thing we can say, without bewilderment or ambiguity—God is here. Like those two disciples when they heard St John the Baptist acclaim the Lamb of God, who should take away the sins of the world, we, taught by the Church that all salvation is to be found in Christ, are eager to know more of him, to see him in the most representative light possible, to catch a glimpse of him in the setting, in the surroundings which most truly manifest his character. "Master," we ask him, "where dost thou live?" And he points to the tabernacle with the invitation, "Come and see."

Let us look at Jesus Christ in his home, in the tabernacle, and see how those surroundings fit him, illustrate his dealings with us. First he dwells in a very public place. The lodging in which the two disciples found our Lord was in the wilderness, perhaps, beyond Jordan; but it was a place of coming and going, for all Jewry went forth to John, we are told, to be baptized by him. Our Lord was near the centre of things, then; and so he is today; in the heart of the greatest city in the world, you can find him without difficulty. So great is his desire to be of use to us that he throws himself in our way, makes himself cheap by familiarity. He is not afraid of irreverence, so long as he can be there when we want him. When they ask us where our God is, we do not have to map out the route of some far pilgrimage in foreign parts; he is close by, at the end of the next street. "O thou whom my soul loves"—we should do ill not to love him, when he makes himself so accessible as that.

Yet he lives there very quietly, a prince in incognito. He walked beyond Jordan for all the world to see; but it was the tenth hour when he invited the two disciples to follow him; it was an evening interview; and it was under cover of night that he talked to Nicodemus. Easy to find out where our Lord dwells; but if we would converse with him, be intimate with him, it must be in the obscurity of faith—the veil of the sacramental species hides him from our sight. He demands something of us after all; we must make a venture of faith in order to find him. So accessible to all, and yet such depths of intimacy for those who will take the trouble to cultivate his friendship!

And when he makes the tabernacle his home he dwells among us very humbly, in great simplicity. St John tells us nothing, as we were complaining just now, about the hospitality he and St Andrew enjoyed that evening. But everything we know about our Lord's life and our Lord's attitude makes us feel certain that it was only a mean

RONALD KNOX

lodging to which he brought them; I picture him as stooping low, and warning them to stoop in their turn, as they entered the door of it. So in the tabernacle he lives a life of utter humility. Oh, we try to make the best of it with gold and marble and precious silk; but he has chosen simple things, common things, to be the hiding-place of his majesty. And as he has stooped, so we must stoop if we are to keep our appointment with him in his favourite meeting-place. We must come to him in abject consciousness of our own unworthiness. For, see, there is something more he wants to tell us about the lodging he has chosen on earth.

Master, where dost thou live? Come and see, he answers—and bids us look into ourselves, into our own souls. It is there that he has chosen his lodging; there, amid all those tainted ambitions and unholy desires, there, in the heart of our warped nature, he dwells in us, and we what we are! Show me where is thy resting-place— heaven knows we need a guide to assure us of it, before we would dare to guess that he is content to dwell *here*.

> If by chance thou e'er shalt doubt
> Where to turn in search of me,
> Seek not all the world about;
> Only this can find me out—
> Thou must seek myself in thee.
> In the mansion of thy mind
> Is my dwelling-place; and more
> There I wander, unconfined,
> Knocking loud if e'er I find
> In thy thought a closed door.

Sacrament Most Holy

A door closed, to him? Not here, Lord, not in these hearts; come, take possession of them, and make them more worthy to be thy home.

V

Giving of Thanks

Not one has come back to give God the praise, except this stranger.
(LUKE 17:18)

THOSE WORDS form the conclusion of a very simple and telling incident in our Lord's life. Ten lepers, isolated by their common calamity from the rest of their kind, cried out to him from a distance asking to be cured. He sent them off to show themselves to the priests, as the law of Moses ordained that a leper should, when there was any doubt about his condition. And as they went, they were cleansed. One of them, it seems, was doubly an untouchable. He was not only a leper, but a Samaritan, hated and distrusted by the Jews among whom he lived, tolerated only by those nine others who were smitten with the same disease. And he, finding himself cured, had other thoughts than to go off at once to the priests and obtain a certificate of his cure. He must go back, and find his benefactor, to cast himself at his feet in gratitude. It was done, and he received the welcome none ever failed to receive from Jesus of Nazareth. But there was a touch of sadness about the words in which it was extended to him. "Were not all ten made clean? And the other

---

Preached during the advance of the Allied armies through Italy.

nine, where are they? Not one has come back to give God the praise, except this stranger." Ten cured, and only one grateful. Nine spoilt children of God's chosen race, cured of their leprosy, and taking it as a matter of course!

I am mentioning this incident for a curious reason; I think it is the only occasion on which you can quote our Lord as insisting on the duty of gratitude. If you look through St Paul's epistles, you will find it dwelt on almost wearisomely; thirty or forty times in the course of them we are reminded that we must, all the time, be giving thanks to God. Yet you will find no phrase expressing gratitude in the Our Father. What will account for this strange difference between the teaching of St Paul and the teaching of his Master? Why, I think you can say this—that our Lord, because he was God, would not be for ever demanding from his creatures the thanks they owed to him. In our common experience, who is it that excites our dislike almost as much as the ungrateful man? Surely the benefactor who is always harping on his benefits and demanding gratitude. So, with that infinite courtesy of his, our Lord would not go about saying, "Be grateful; whatever you do, remember to be grateful." He would leave us to find out *that*, at least, for ourselves; he would trust poor, wounded human nature to retain at least that grace, if it had nothing else left to it—the grace of gratitude.

I have said that St Paul is constantly recurring to this thought; let us not forget to notice that the word he uses for gratitude is *eucharistia*. And when, as often happens, he couples the notion with that of prayer, when he says, for example, to the Philippians, "make your requests known to God, praying and beseeching him, and giving him thanks as well" (Phil. 4:6), it is not by any means clear that he is not referring, at least by implication, to the sacrament of Holy Eucharist. For this, it is certain, is one of the earliest titles by which that greatest of all sacraments was known to Christian thought. "By prayer and supplication, together with the offering of the Holy Eucharist, let your petitions be known unto God"—that gives the sentence, it must be admitted, a more familiar turn. But, always, the notion of gratitude is there. And rightly so, naturally so; for this sacrament is by its very title, in its very origin, a sacrament of thanksgiving.

How often did our Lord himself publicly offer thanks to God? Only three times, as far as our records enlighten us. He gave thanks to God at those two great miracles, the feeding of the five thousand and the raising of Lazarus. And he gave thanks to God once more when he was about to perform the greatest of all his miracles; when he stood there in the cenacle, on the night on which he was betrayed, ready to turn the substance of bread and wine into that of his adorable body and blood. In all three gospels that record the scene, and equally in the account of which St Paul gives us, that detail is prominent; he gave thanks, and broke the bread; he gave thanks, and bade them drink of the cup. Even now the chief priests are making ready for his arrest, and he knows it. Even now the traitor is sitting with him at table, and he knows it. But the thought which fills the heart of our divine Lord at that first Mass of Christendom is an overwhelming impulse of gratitude.

How strange, that when you read the ordinary kind of instruction you get about the Mass, so little is said about this primitive, this dominating aspect of it! You will be told that in the Mass we offer praise to God; that is implied in all sacrifice. You will be told

Sacrament Most Holy

that in the Mass we offer reparation for our sins; we are not likely to forget that. You will be told that in the Mass we offer petition for our own needs and the needs of all Christians, living and dead; the very urgency of those needs is clamorous in our minds, threatens, almost, to be a distraction. But how little they insist that at the Holy Eucharist we ought to be giving thanks to God, because that is what the word "Eucharist" means!

It is not the liturgy that is at fault. For, if you will examine the familiar words of it, you will find that everywhere praise and thanksgiving are inextricably mingled. When we praise God, we think of what he is in himself, high above us, infinitely greater than we are, wholly independent of us. But in the same breath we thank him for what he is to *us*, what he does for *us*. "We praise thee, we bless thee, we adore thee, we glorify thee, we give thanks to thee in the greatness of thy glory." So, in the *Gloria*, we dispose ourselves for sacrifice; and when the sacrifice proper begins, we allow ourselves, for the moment, to forget even the duty of praising God, so overwhelmed are we by the thought of his benefits to us. "Let us give thanks to the Lord our God.… It is fitting, it is right so to do.… Indeed it is fitting, it is right, it is to be expected of us, it is our hope of salvation, that always and everywhere we should give thee thanks." For every mystery of our faith, from our Lady's child-bearing to the expectation of the faithful dead, it is always thanks we offer to God, just here. And when we reach the solemn moment of consecration, the liturgy does not forget to echo the overtones of Maundy Thursday. "Lifting up his hands to thee, his almighty Father, he gave thanks and blessed, and broke." "Taking this glorious cup into his holy and worshipful hands, he gave thanks to thee again, and blessed, and gave." Even when he communicates, the priest has to keep the same thought in mind. He has already received the sacred host, and you would expect him to drink the precious blood immediately afterwards. But no, a kind of scruple seems to occur to him, and make him hesitate. "What can I do for the Lord," he asks himself, "*in return* for all that he has done for me?" He will make sure, before he completes the sacrifice, that it is a sacrifice of thanksgiving from first to last.

The reason for that is not far to seek. In the Mass, helpless man is trying to hide away, to compensate for, the utter worthlessness of his own aspirations towards God, by uniting them to the perfect aspirations of the God-Man here offered up in sacrifice. Sinful creatures, we have neither the status nor the capacity to make any worthy oblation. We *want* to praise God, but what do our earth-bound minds know of his greatness? And what is our praise worth? No, we will leave it to Jesus Christ; he shall praise God for us. We want forgiveness, but what title have we to obtain it? We will burden the divine victim with the weight of our sins; he shall lay them at our Father's feet for us, and be told that they are forgiven. We want so many graces and favours, for ourselves and for others; but do we know what is best, for ourselves or for them? And if we did, have we the effrontery to make any demands before the throne we have so often rebelled against? No, we will put it all in our Lord's hands, make him our plenipotentiary and let him act for us, win for us just the graces and the favours he wants us to have.

And so it is with our thanksgiving. We might have been inclined to suggest that here, at least, we could trust ourselves to do our duty unaided. Surely the very consciousness of our own inadequacy,

Sacrament Most Holy

which makes us so eager to find an intermediary with God, should have the effect of enhancing our gratitude; that he should have mercies to spare for people like us, gifts to bestow on people like us! But no; once more we are not competent even to thank God as he deserves to be thanked. How little we know, really, of what he does for us! How often we may have been within an ace of death, and we none the wiser! How often we have been preserved from the temptation that might have proved too strong for us, and we never knew that it was there! Even if we knew how good he has been to us, have we the apparatus for feeling, still more for showing, the gratitude which that goodness deserves? You have seen, before now, a present given to a child which is only just beginning to speak; how it will gaze at the toy with obvious pleasure, but never once look up into the eyes of the person who gave it, as if there were any connection between giver and gift. You know how the mother has to elicit a decent appearance of gratitude from her child, while she herself, really, has to do all the thanking there is to be done.... If we could see the Holy Eucharist at work, as the angels see it, I wonder if that isn't the light in which we should see our gratitude, and Christ's?

Thanksgiving, then, must be added to praise, reparation and intercession as an integral part of the Christian sacrifice, as one of its chief ends. And among these four ends it takes the second place. Praise comes first, because we praise God in himself without any thought of our own interest. Thanksgiving next—it comes before reparation for our sins, because, sinful creatures though we are, we are creatures before we are sinners; it comes before intercession, because justice demands that we should thank God for what he has done for us before we ask him to do more. God wants us to ask for his favours. But he wants us first to assure him of our loving gratitude for the past. Many of you will know, at least by seeing reproductions of it, Michelangelo's picture of the creation of Adam, in the Sistine Chapel at Rome. You will remember that recumbent figure, stretching out one hand, at the full length of the arm, towards the Creator, as if in acknowledgment of its utter dependence, its creaturely reliance, on him. That attitude, that eucharistic attitude, should be at the roots of all our devotion to almighty God. It should be in our thoughts at all times; it should be in our thoughts especially when we assist at Holy Mass, or when we see, throned above the altar, that body which is our victim in the Holy Mass. And when, from time to time, the consciousness of some great mercy strikes across our lives, it should intensify this eucharistic attitude in us, turn us into living flames of thankfulness; *Dignum et justum est*, we should cry out, uniting our voices with those of the blessed angels in heaven, "It is fitting and right, almighty, eternal God, that we should always and everywhere give thanks to thee."

When we say a Mass of thanksgiving, we say the Mass of Trinity Sunday. And, this Trinity Sunday, a great load of anxiety has been lifted from the minds of civilized people all over the world. It was not merely that Rome passed, overnight, into the hands of the Allied Powers, though that in itself was matter enough for gratitude. It was the first capital of a European nation that has been won by our arms. And there is finality about the very name of Rome; those of us who remember the last war could not help being reminded of a similar omen, when General Allenby's troops captured Jerusalem in September 1918. But there was more in it than that. If Rome, the capital of all our fortunes, was to be won, could it be

Sacrament Most Holy

won, standing? Or would we see pictures of it lying in the dust, like the Abbey of Monte Cassino? In that city, isolated from the ambitions, but not from the perils that surrounded him, lived the ruler of a great spiritual empire, the personification of a great spiritual ideal. Was he to see the city he loved wrecked, amid the wreck of the world he loved? We know the answer. Rome stands; and Adam, on the ceiling of the Sistine Chapel, stretches out his hand towards the Creator, unharmed as when Michelangelo drew him, more than four hundred years ago.

VI

As Your Servant

Blessed are those servants, whom their master will find watching when he comes; I promise you, he will gird himself, and make them sit down to meat, and minister to them. (LUKE 12:43)

HOW OLD-FASHIONED the setting of our Lord's parables look to us nowadays! We have forgotten even what it was to stay in a large house with half a dozen servants to look after it; and our Lord is speaking of slaves. A slave did not expect much; our Lord has given us elsewhere what was obviously a familiar picture of a farm servant coming in from a hard day's work, and being told to wait on his master before he got a meal himself. Here, he is giving us what is obviously an unfamiliar picture, that of a master waiting on his servants.

The Master waiting on his servants—as if to assure his disciples that the Holy Eucharist was a foretaste of heaven, we know what our Lord did. At the Last Supper he knelt down and washed their feet. And when he came to St Peter—last of all, I suppose; that seems to have been the spirit of the occasion—St Peter made the obvious protest, "Lord, is it for *thee* to wash *my* feet?" The disciples, you will remember, had just been having a discussion among themselves, which should be the greatest. It seems an inappropriate moment,

Sacrament Most Holy

but St Luke assures us that it was so. And our Lord solved the difficulty by asking them, "Tell me, which is the greater, the man who sits at table, or the man who serves him? Surely the man who sits at table, yet I am here among you as your servant" (Luke 22:27). Then he suits the action to the word; girds himself like a slave and kneels with a basin at their feet. Oh yes, Peter is to be the greatest among them; but when he achieves that position, it will not be long before he realizes what it involves; to be the chief Christian is to be *servus servorum Dei*, slave of the slaves of God.

Our Lord does not say, "Look at me, watch what I am doing at this moment; see how, when need arises, I can abase myself." He says, "I am here among you as your servant"—it is not a mere momentary gesture; what he says of himself is true all the time. I am here among you, here on earth, among you men; there would be no point in God becoming Man, unless he who was fashioned in the likeness of men went further, and took upon himself the form of a slave. The whole process of the Incarnation, if you come to think of it, is a topsy-turvy kind of arrangement; it is God doing something for the sake of man, when man only exists for the sake of God.

He came to earth, and lived for the sake of us men. Oh, to be sure, the first motive in every action of his was to please his heavenly Father; "I must do the will of him who sent me" (John 6:38). But that general resolve does not exclude the influence of ordinary human motives, "I am sorry for the multitude, because they have nothing to eat" (Mark 8:2). It wouldn't be true of our Lord to say that he never did anything for his own comfort or content. He did sit down and rest by Jacob's well; he did go to sleep in the boat when he was tired out; he did steal away onto the mountain-side by himself, when everybody was looking for him and he could get no time for prayer. Even more noticeably, he did allow other people to do things for him, and accepted their good offices with gratitude; he let the Magdalen anoint him, and Simon help to carry his cross, and at the last moment of his life he, who had been nursed at a human mother's breast, would slake his thirst with a little wine, accepting the rough charity of his executioner. But the whole nature of his career marks it out for what we are accustomed to call it—a ministry. The long lines of eager suppliants, demanding health, repulsive in their very importunity; the burning glare of publicity, without a platform, without an orator's privileges, so that every foolish criticism must be weighed and answered; the complete condescension to the ordinary man's level, so that every chance comer can pluck you by the sleeve, instead of waiting in an ante-room to gain admission—all *that*, as anybody will tell you who has had, even in a small way, an experience of the limelight, means a constant drain on the vitality, a constant sense of virtue having gone out of you, which makes a man the victim of his audience. And then there were the apostles—honest, warm-hearted men, but, until he had finished with them, how slow and stupid! A schoolmaster, if he is a good schoolmaster, must needs be a servant, and almost a drudge; in that drudgery, how much of our Lord's earthly life was spent!

Propter nos homines—if that was true of his life on earth as Man, it is equally true of the sacramental life which continues it. Why do we not have those words written up over every tabernacle? Here is God, if we may dare to put it in that way, at the beck and call of us men. Oh, it is true that in all the sacraments you have a direct impact of God's power on human lives. It's only because we

Sacrament Most Holy

are so incorrigibly spoilt that we *will* think of the sacraments as if they were laid on, and nothing remained for us to do except turn a tap. No, God is present in all his sacraments, if we like to think of it in that way. But, as if to cure us of our stupidity, he would honour us by a special kind of presence in the Blessed Sacrament of the altar. Our Lord should be present as Man, for the sake of us men; putting himself at our disposal whenever we wanted him, making himself available for every purpose for which we want him, like a servant who says to his master, "Here I am; what do you want of me?"

Putting himself at our disposal—what a lot of difference there is between the servant who is always there and the old lady who will come in sometimes to oblige! If our Lord consented to be present once a year, at one particular altar in the world, what a condescension it would be! And here he is, always at our elbow. Making himself available—how grateful we are to the servant who is ready to take on unaccustomed duties in an emergency, instead of saying, "That isn't my place!" And our Lord is ready to meet all our needs, chime in with all our moods, from the day of our first communion to the day when we receive him in Viaticum. Always waiting there in silence, not pressing his services upon us, but ready if we want him. What a poor idea we form of the man who passes over a service without gratitude, because a fellow man has rendered it so unobtrusively! And yet we go on from day to day, forgetting the unobtrusive service of a God.

See how he stoops, when he comes to a child in its first communion! The priest himself must stoop, almost ridiculously, to reach the tiny figure that has to stand upright if he is to reach it at all. And this posture of the priest, which itself, somehow, brings tears to the eye, is but the outward image of the unbelievable condescension involved on the part of his divine Master. Can we really believe that he had this sort of thing in mind when he instituted the Holy Eucharist? It is meant to be the bread of the strong, the day's rations for the campaigner in life's battle; a child like this, not yet capable (it is to be supposed) of sinning mortally, does not take the strain of conflict, does not need, therefore, supernatural refreshment. St Paul tells us that the communicant eats and drinks unworthily, if he does not recognize the Lord's body for what it is—can this child of five years old really grasp anything about eucharistic doctrine, beyond the fact that what he is receiving now is mysteriously different from his everyday food? Are we not presuming too much on the condescension of the Incarnate, when we throw open his mysteries to such under-developed spirituality as this?

So men thought, so even Catholics thought, till yesterday; and God had to raise up a saint to show us that we were wrong; had to raise him up, under the title of Pius the Tenth, to the throne of Peter, before we could realize that we were wrong. "It is not for thee to know *now* what I am doing, but thou wilt understand it afterwards" (John 7:13); so our Lord spoke when Peter was bewildered by the condescension of Maundy Thursday, and the lesson was not fully learned for eighteen centuries. But we *ought* to have known; had not this same divine Master said, "Let the children be, do not keep them back from me; the kingdom of heaven belongs to such as these" (Matt. 19:14)? Evil as we are, we know well enough how to give our children what is good for them; if a child falls sick, we all turn hospital nurse; if a child is in danger, we compete for the honour of rescuing it; and should our Lord care less for children

Sacrament Most Holy

than we? *Propter nos homines*, for us human beings, children as well as men; the more he stoops, the better he is pleased.

See how he stoops, when he comes to a dying man in holy Viaticum! Those poor wandering wits, that cannot string a coherent sentence together to take leave of us, who knew him so well—have they really enough powers of concentration left to be called properly alive? The trembling fingers move as if to make the sign of the cross, but is that more than a kind of automatic gesture? Is it really directed by the tired brain? Absolution, yes, to be sure, on the chance that there is still time for a change of heart so momentous; extreme unction, oil knows how to consecrate even lifeless things. But, the Holy Eucharist—to receive that, we must surely be at our best! Is it kind in us to demand effort, perhaps to awaken scruples, in the soul that is so nearly cut loose from its last anchorage? But, even as we hesitate, a gracious Figure brushes us aside, still bent on his errand of mercy: "The child is not dead, she is asleep.... Our friend Lazarus is at rest now; I am going there to awake him" (Mark 5:39; John 11:11). *Propter nos homines*; the dying man can do so little for himself; because he cannot come to our Lord, our Lord comes to him.

"Why then, if I have washed your feet, I who am the Master and the Lord, you in your turn ought to wash one another's feet." When next we find ourselves refusing service to a fellow man, let us remember who it was that came to us this morning, and woke us from our sleep, and asked what orders we had for him.

VII

The Gleaner

*Listen, my daughter, Booz said to Ruth; do not look
for any other field to glean in.* (RUTH 2:8)

MAY I REMIND YOU—it is well for us to be reminded sometimes about the less read parts of Holy Scripture—of the story told in the book of Ruth?

Noemi, a woman of Bethlehem, went to live in the land of Moab. Her husband died there, leaving two sons; these married Moabite wives, and died also, leaving, it seems, no children. Noemi then returned to the land of Juda, accompanied by her two daughters-in-law; she pressed them to go back to their own kindred, and one of them, Orpha, at last consented, but Ruth stuck close to her mother-in-law. "I mean to go where thou goest, and dwell where thou dwellest; thy people shall be my people, thy God my God; whatever earth closes over thee when thou diest shall be my place of death and burial. Due meed of punishment the Lord give me, and more than due, if aught but death part thee and me" (Ruth 1:16–17).

They came to Bethlehem, then, together. They were poor, and Ruth went out to glean in a rich man's field—she was allowed, for charity, to follow behind the reapers and pick up the stray handsful

Sacrament Most Holy

of corn they had left behind them. Without knowing it, she followed the reapers in a field which belonged to Booz, who was her own kinsman. He, recognizing her, encouraged her to remain with his reapers, "Daughter, do not go to glean in any other field"; and he gave secret directions to his own servants, telling them to leave generous store for her to gather as she followed them. At last they made themselves known to each other, and Booz claimed her hand in marriage. And so it was that Ruth, the woman of Moab, became the ancestress of St Joseph, of our blessed Lady, and, according to the flesh, of our Lord Jesus Christ himself.

A remote story of days long dead, touching in its simplicity, a favourite subject for the painter and for the poet—but what has it all to do with us? What message has it for us, children of a less lovable age? I never realized how plain was the symbolism of it until I came across a chapter in an old-fashioned book of meditations from the French, headed "The Field of the Holy Eucharist."

After all, do they differ so much from ourselves, those two daughters-in-law of the exiled Jewess Noemi? Do they not represent two different types of soul, the soul which chooses and the soul which forsakes the world, the soul which is false and the soul which is true to its supernatural loyalties? The memory of a dead husband, what power has it to chain the affections, to spoil the life of a woman still young and still beautiful, as Orpha was, or Ruth? Yet Ruth was loyal to the country of her adoption, the country she had never seen; an Israelite by marriage, she would become an Israelite by choice. "Whither thou goest, I will go; thy people shall be my people, and thy God my God." So the faithful soul hears two voices, the flattering accents of the world at its elbow, the distant call of its unseen, because supernatural, home. Will it throw in its lot with the Christian Church, its mother by adoption, or will it go back to the world which claims it by right of natural kinship? The Church does not make it easy for us; she makes exacting demands of us, she tests our loyalty. "Go back," she says, "unless you are prepared to throw in your lot with mine for better or worse." And the faithful soul still answers, "Due meed of punishment the Lord give me, and more than due, if aught but death part thee and me."

And so she brings us to Bethlehem, to the house of bread. She brings us to the altar, where he who is our kinsman by right of his Incarnation, he who would espouse our souls to himself through divine charity, hides himself from us and bids us glean what we may in the field of the Holy Eucharist. His field, for who bought it, who sowed it, who cultivated it, if not he? He bought it by his Incarnation; being rich, he became poor for our sakes; he sold all that he had, and bought that field. He sowed it, by his death; "a grain of wheat must fall into the ground and die, or else it remains nothing more than a grain of wheat; but if it dies, then it yields rich fruit" (John 12:24–25); his own sacred body was the seed, committed to the tomb that it might live with a new life. He cultivated the field by all the merits of his life and Passion; it was watered by the tears which he shed over Jerusalem, by his sweat in Gethsemani, by the blood of his scourging. And as, by a miracle of nature, one seed multiplies itself, till the harvest far exceed the measure of those grain from which it sprang, so from that one sacred body, that was sown in tears by the rock-tomb on Calvary, sprang a harvest world-wide, incalculable, inexhaustible, the harvest of the holy Eucharist; millions of Hosts in thousands of tabernacles all over the

Sacrament Most Holy

world. The harvest which was sown in tears on Maundy Thursday is reaped with joy on Corpus Christi. That is what the feast of Corpus Christi is, our spiritual harvest home. Pentecost, for the Jews, was a harvest festival, and we, when we have kept our Pentecost, carry in triumph through field and hedgerow that consecrated sheaf which is the harvest of Calvary. See how they shine today, those myriad Hosts of the world, in the sun of Eastertide, swayed as if by the wind of Pentecost.

In that field of the Holy Eucharist you and I are gleaners. Gleaners—why not reapers? Would that we were reapers; but look into your heart, and ask whether gleaning is not the true description for those poor, half-hearted crumbs of devotion which you and I carry away with us from God's altar. Imagine what Ruth must have felt as she watched the servants of Booz, lifting great armfuls of the wheat and binding them together, while she herself might only pick up, here and there, a stray wisp or two dropped from careless hands. How sadly she must have followed them with her eyes, she, no better than a supernumerary and a hanger-on! So you and I, when we read the lives of the saints, follow, with a wistful regret that tries not to be envy, the account of those spiritual privileges they received when they came to the altar. St Philip Neri, with his daily hours of ecstasy. The Little Flower at her first communion. "Jesus asked nothing of me, and claimed no sacrifice. That day our meeting was more than simple recognition, it was perfect union. We were no longer two; Thérèse had disappeared like a drop of water lost in the immensity of the ocean"—her first communion; and have you and I, after so many years spent in frequenting the sacraments, had an experience to match that?

RONALD KNOX

Yes, it is the saints who reap; you and I are only gleaners in their track. You come into church, and, just for a moment or two, the coolness and the retirement of it compose your mind for holy thoughts; you begin to pray. And then, at the most improbable tangent of thought, by the most grotesque association of ideas, your attention wanders to some detail of your daily life, some anxiety that troubles you, some pleasure you forecast, some ambition you cherish...why, here is the Gospel being said already, and no prayers yet! A fresh effort, a little more recollection, and then some oddity of manner about the priest, some eccentricity in your neighbour's deportment, carries you off again into profitless speculations; it is only the bell ringing for the consecration that brings you back, with a shock, to the sense of where you are, what you are doing. "My Lord and my God!" In five minutes from now, you are to receive him, your God and your all, into the hospitality of this distracted soul. Well, it is done somehow; and some affections of love and gratitude spring, as if unbidden, from the heart; and then all at once you find yourself fidgeting, your eyes straying to take a peep at your watch, and so you leave the church again. My daughter, my daughter, where hast thou gleaned today?

Would it not be better, you ask yourself sometimes, to give up the idea of frequent communion? Without abandoning your religious duties to transfer your inmost loyalties elsewhere; to fix your ambitions, as others do, on worldlier objects? There are other fields, oh yes, which promise some kind of satisfaction besides the field of the Holy Eucharist; the pursuit of power, or of human wisdom, or of riches, or of pleasure—would you not be better employed over one of these? It is so hard to be always doing

Sacrament Most Holy

a thing, and always doing it badly. And then it is that the Celestial Husbandman says to you, "Daughter, do not go to glean in any other field." Wherever we turn, whatever field of activity we choose for ourselves, you and I will only be gleaners still. Are we ambitious? Then see how few posts there are in the world by which ambition can really be gratified; others will reap the reward, we shall only be allowed to glean as best we may in their track. Do we desire knowledge, would we wrest from Nature yet more of her secrets? Then see, how many have been in the field before us; how they have swept it bare, and only left to us a few undistinguished avenues of research. Or would we fall back on the vulgar pursuit of riches? Here, too, we are too late in the field; others have been beforehand with us, have scraped up all the prizes, and left only the gleanings of their harvest for us who follow them. Would we live for mere pleasures? Why, this is a more pathetic fallacy than the rest! For who that ever asked for pleasure, ever devoted his life to pleasure, found that he could fill his bosom with its grudging sheaves? No, pleasures themselves are only the stray pickings of life to be gleaned by the wayside; there is no satisfying yourself with them. Daughter, do not go to glean, for thou canst do no more than glean, in any other field but mine!

Booz, when he saw that Ruth was following with his reapers, gave them special directions concerning her. "They were to put no hindrance in her way, though she were to go reaping in their company; and of set purpose they were to drop some of the handfuls they gathered, and leave them there for her to glean" (Ruth 2:15–16). What other householder would so have instructed his servants? And who but our blessed Lord would have left to us, his

49

indevout worshippers, gleanings so rich from his all-sufficing harvest? Those wayward thoughts of ours, those wandering prayers—what sort of blessing could we expect that they would call down from above? We are not worthy of the least of his mercies, and he gives us—himself! In that Host which was carried round St Peter's this morning, with princes of the Church for its escort, with multitudes adoring on every side, there was not more of Christ than in the Host which this morning the priest laid upon your tongue. In the Host with which Soeur Thérèse was given her first communion there was not more of Christ than in the Host which you receive, week by week, day by day. It is not his generosity that is wanting, if we glean so little from his harvest; it is ours.

Glean on, then, faithful soul, in the field of Jesus Christ. He has sent us, he himself says, to reap that whereon we bestowed no labour; he ploughed, he sowed, he cultivated that harvest which he bids us gather day by day; no root of grace has ever sprouted since the hour of his crucifixion which has not owed, to that momentous act of charity, its origin and its value. It was the curse of fallen man that he should eat bread in the sweat of his brow; nor has our redemption lifted from us, so far as our natural needs are concerned, the weight of that sentence; we must labour, must suffer, must be anxious still. But the supernatural grace which the redemption won for us comes to us all unsought, all unbought, thrusts itself upon us, lies scattered in our way. And, above all, the grace of the Holy Eucharist, no transient influence of the divine mercy, but God himself, is lavished upon us with reckless bounty; we have but to stoop to gather it, and it is ours! What, glean in any other field, when the heavenly manna, the bread of angels, offers itself to our taste?

Sacrament Most Holy

With happy significance, this church of Corpus Christi lies close to one of the busiest thoroughfares of the world's greatest city. Day in, day out, to and fro, these pavements are trodden by the hurrying footsteps of men and women going forth to earn their daily bread. Towering hotels offer to the traveller, at fantastic prices, a night's lodging. And here, thrust into their midst, a Catholic church, the depository and the namesake of a treasure greater than any merit of man could earn, preaches its dumb message of refreshment and repose. "It is but lost labour that ye rise up so early, and so late take rest, and eat the bread of carefulness, for so he giveth his beloved sleep." Ruth, when her long day of gleaning was over, lay down at the feet of Booz, her protector; and when morning came he awoke, and claimed her for himself. So we, when the day's burden and its heats are done, will lay ourselves down at the feet of him whom we adore in this most august sacrament; and we shall awake to see his face in the clear air of morning, and be united with him for evermore.

VIII

Peace in Ourselves

*That they too may be one in us, as thou, Father,
art in me, and I in thee.* (JOHN 17:21)

OUR LORD, on the eve of his Passion, quoted the words, "I will smite the shepherd, and the sheep shall be scattered" (Matt. 26:31). The prospect of being deserted by his apostles in the hour of danger does not fill him with a sense of loneliness; he is well prepared to face, alone, the false verdict, and the mockery, and the shame of crucifixion. The tragedy is rather that these friends of his, who for three years past have been united in so close a bond of companionship, because they were his friends, are to lose that centre of common loyalty, and be scattered every man to his own. The compact little society will become a rabble of self-contained units, each fending for itself; the link that bound them together will have gone. Somehow, we do not know why, man is born for fellowship, and the breaking-up of any human circle demands its tribute of tears. By way of fortifying their human hearts, fortifying, perhaps, his own human heart against the strain of this parting, our Lord prays such a prayer as no merely human leader would have ventured to

---

This sermon was written just after the end of hostilities in Europe.

Sacrament Most Holy

conceive. He prays that the disciples may be one with that very unity which binds together the three persons of the Godhead itself.

And we, year by year, recall to ourselves that prayer of his by celebrating two feasts in close conjunction. The Thursday after Trinity Sunday is for us what you might call Unity Thursday; we keep the festival of Corpus Christi, and in doing so we cast our minds back to the upper room and the first Eucharist, when our Lord incorporated his friends into a society by incorporating them into himself. Always the liturgy remembers what we, who use the liturgy, are so prone to forget—that the Holy Eucharist is a sacrament of unity. When the consecration takes place, what happens? The substance of the bread and wine is withdrawn from them; the accidents remain. And yet, in our ordinary experience, it is the substance and the substance alone which lends any natural thing its unity. Shape and size and colour and smell and the resistance which it offers to the touch come together in a single principle of unity, the substance; it is the linch-pin which holds them all in place. Take away the linch-pin, and the wheel flies off. Take away the substance, and, by a miracle, so stupendous that our minds can hardly conceive it, the accidents do not fall apart; they remain there to be the garment and the vehicle of a quite different and a far greater substance, that of our Lord's own body and blood. His word upholds them; the same word which prayed, at the Last Supper, that the apostles might remain one; might remain one, even when their Master, the focus of loyalty by which their fellowship maintained itself, was taken away. The unity which unites three persons in one Godhead, the unity which preserves in being a set of accidents which have lost their substance—that is the unity we Christians pray for, and claim as our own when we gather round our Father's table at the Holy Eucharist.

Again and again you will find the language of the sacred liturgy dominated by this idea of oneness in Christ; a supernatural oneness which triumphs over every disparity, every separation. That is, I think, the idea which underlies one of the most beautiful, and at the same time one of the most obscure, petitions which we make during Lent; when we ask almighty God *ut congregata restaures, et restaurata conserves*, "that thou wouldst bring together and mend, mend and for ever preserve, what now lies broken." Bring together and mend, mend and for ever preserve, what now lies broken—is it possible not to feel like that about the cruel divisions introduced into the world, into states, into families by these six years of war? So many millions of men torn away from their homes; and of these a great number, even now, unable to go home because circumstances have changed at home, and they find themselves outlaws. So many nations torn by bitter internal feuds, that will hardly be healed in our lifetime. And the world in general so weary of war, and yet so far from the very elements of harmony, so ignorant of the very alphabet of peace! "That thou wouldst bring together and mend, mend and for ever preserve, what now lies broken"—do we not need that prayer, when we see the mortar of civilization cracking all around us?

Congregata restaures, et restaurata conserves; the Church, knowing well what we are, members of a fallen race, does not simply ask God to keep us in our present position, and leave it at that. She

---

1. *Oratio super Populum* for the third Thursday of Lent.

Sacrament Most Holy

knows that *that* will not do, we are scattered all over the place, like broken pieces of china, and we have got to be put together again before we can be worth preserving. No, we must not be so miserably small-minded in our prayers as to tell God that we want him to keep the world just as it is, a mass of quarrels and seething discontents, if only we can have five or ten years of peace before hostilities start again. We must ask him to gather up the broken pieces of our world and cement them together again in some kind of world order, based on real justice, to give Europe statesmen who will keep their word and will grant freedom to their fellow countrymen, before we can ask him to keep things as they are.

But there is more behind it. If we will be honest with ourselves, we shall admit that the war has brought disharmony into your life and mine; we are not at peace in ourselves. Most of us are much busier than we used to be; in days when labour is short, we have more things to do; in days when the necessities of life are harder to come by, we have more things to think about. The great cruelties, the great injustices we read about in the newspapers rankle in our minds, and turn the milk of human kindness bitter within us. We shrink from the novel experiment of building a new world on the ruins of the old; we are sad at the disappearance of old landmarks, uneasy at the changes in our familiar habits of life. Travel is more difficult and more wearisome; we find it hard to make contact with old friends, even when we are little divided from them by distance. All *that* sets up a restlessness in our minds which perhaps is good for us in a way; it may save us from falling too much into a rut and taking life too easily. But it does not make the business of our souls a more encouraging task. For that, we need tranquillity, recollection; how are we to think about God or eternity, with daily needs and worldly preoccupations and public cares so weighing on our minds? The thought of God seems to get crowded out; our own sins get overlooked—they are so petty, compared with the needs of a distracted world, the perils of an uncertain future. While the war was still close to us, and danger seemed imminent, we could fix our minds on the common effort, forget the future and everything that was not part of our own immediate job. Now, the strain has relaxed, but our thoughts are still over-occupied. They rattle through your head as the rosary-beads rattle between your fingers; you feel as if you were not one person, but a mass of whirling fantasies, of disconnected trains of speculation.

Not one person, but a mass of fantasies—haven't we got back again to the need for unity? Aren't we conscious, once again, of the need for praying that almighty God will bring together and mend, mend and for ever preserve, what now lies broken? Haven't we got to be at peace within ourselves before we can bring any peace to the world in which we live? Instead of that, we lose our heads, take counsel of the prejudice that is uppermost, and make hasty decisions. We get irritable, and give way to depressions and despairs. How are we going to introduce any singleness of purpose into our lives, any recollection and repose into our thoughts?

You will learn to integrate yourself, pull yourself together, in the way we are speaking of, precisely in proportion as you manage to get more closely in touch, and more intimately in touch, with the eucharistic life of our blessed Lord. The Blessed Sacrament is the sacrament of unity; and when you receive it, it does not merely produce in you more charity towards your neighbour, more loyalty

Sacrament Most Holy

towards the Church, more unselfishness in your human attachments. It makes you more at unity with yourself; it catches up your life into a rhythm that echoes the heavenly music. Strange if it were not so; as we have seen, this presence which comes to you in holy communion comes to you veiled under the accidents of bread and wine, accidents which have now no substance to support them; it reigns amidst chaos, and will it not reign amidst the chaos of your heart? It comes to you, since our Lord's prayer could not go unanswered, full of that unifying love which is the bond of the blessed Trinity, and will it not bring unity into your scattered thoughts, your conflicting ambitions?

Only, there is something to be done on our side. The wheat must be ground into bread, the wine must be pressed out of the grape, before we can give our Lord the opportunity to work his miracle of transubstantiation. The offertory first, man stretching out his hands to God; then the consecration, God accepting and transforming man's gift. We must come to meet him, come to meet him early in the morning, when sleep has smoothed away for us the memories of yesterday, and no cares have yet assailed us to disturb the equilibrium of our lives. We must hand over the direction of our lives to him, if we are to know what it means to live an ordered life, heart-whole and mind-whole in a world like ours. Then we can go to communion.

IX

The Mass and the Ritual

As Christ comes into the world, he says, No sacrifice, no offering was thy demand; thou hast endowed me, instead, with a body.
(HEB. 10:5)

I SUPPOSE ANY IMPARTIAL OBSERVER, comparing the religious ceremonies of the Jews with ours, would be struck by this fact—that the Jews expressed their religion in sacrifices, and we in sacraments. And he would notice this, that whereas sacrifice means the destruction of the body—the body of a bull or a goat or a lamb, substituted by a kind of legal fiction to redeem the body of the man who offers it—our Christian sacraments do not mean the destruction of the body at all. They mean, rather, the consecration of our bodies to God, with the understanding that such consecration symbolizes, and effects, a consecration of our souls as well. God in Christ has abolished the old, destructive sacrifices; he has prepared for us instead a redeemed body in which and through which the sanctification of our souls can take place. The body is washed, and the soul is made clean; the body is anointed, and the soul is strengthened; a little circle of gold is put round one finger, or the hands are tied with a plain strip of linen, and the soul enters, thereupon, into a new state of life.

Sacrament Most Holy

Consider how, at the three most solemn moments of his career, the ordinary Christian comes before God to receive the sacramental grace which those moments require, and can take upon his lips, without irreverence, the very words which our Lord himself uses in the greatest of all his sacraments, *Hoc est corpus meum*—This is my body.

The infant presents itself before God at the font with the words, *Hoc est corpus meum*, this is my body. What other words can it use? There is no other thought of which it can be directly conscious. The troubled eyes, looking out on a world altogether strange to it, are already beginning to isolate one set of phenomena from the rest, those white things, its own hands and feet. If one of those white things comes in contact with the edge of the cradle, feeling results, feeling that communicates itself to the mind; somehow, then, these white things are part of itself. The first judgment we are capable of making is simply the identification of the body as something belonging to us; *hoc est corpus meum*. Soul is there, to be sure, as well as body, in the newly born infant; but the soul has not yet found its own means of expression, has not yet begun to grasp life by experience; it is dumb, inarticulate, has not reached the knowledge of itself. The body is something that has already begun to be known; that, then, must be offered to God, and that is enough; God will cleanse and sanctify this new soul, enable it to partake of eternal life, through the body which he has prepared for it.

Man and woman present themselves before the altar to dedicate their lives in mutual fidelity; and once again it is the body that is uppermost in our thoughts. *Hoc est corpus meum*, the bridegroom says to the bride; with my body I thee worship. For here it is, in the fullness of its powers, that body which was carried, years before, tiny and helpless to the font. It is strong enough to work, now, and to make a livelihood for itself; and not for itself only, but for a household. It is strong enough to defend others besides itself against attack. And it is capable now, if God so wills, of continuing its kind, of begetting fresh life. With all these powers the bridegroom does worship to the bride; yet these are only the symbol of that love whose true sphere is in the soul. And the bride in her turn puts out her finger to receive the ring; *hoc est corpus meum*, she seems to say, here is my body, for you to hold it prisoner; yet her soul goes out with it. As they offer the bodies he has prepared for them to him and to one another, God finds his opportunity to breathe sacramental grace into their souls.

And once again, at the last scene of all, when a man lies on his death-bed, it is through his body that sacramental grace comes to heal him. His body is closer to him than ever; he is conscious of little except its labouring breath, its fevered pulses—this body of which he must take leave so soon, this body which now means so little. *Hoc est corpus meum*, he says, this is my body, still mine for a little, before it returns to its parent earth. This is my body, in which I have taken such pride, to which I have devoted so much attention, in which and through which I have sinned. This is my body; come, holy oil, and anoint it—these eyes that have seen and coveted what was unlawful, these ears that have been open to evil communications, these lips that have lied, detracted, blasphemed, these hands and feet that have been the ministers of my wicked passions. This is my body, which will soon be cold clay, now giving access to my soul, for the last time, through the gateways of sense; let these last

Sacrament Most Holy

sense-impressions of mine be all of holy things; seal them, holy oil, and shut them against the echoes of earth. So God's grace comes to him, for the last time, through his body, and his soul is healed.

We Christians, then, can offer our bodies to God, a reasonable, living sacrifice; but only for one reason. Only because God himself was made flesh, took upon himself a passible body like ours, offered it at every moment of his life to his heavenly Father, was born in it, laboured in it, suffered in it, died in it. He wore that body in its state of infancy, humiliated, annihilated for our sakes.... This is my body, for you, my mother, to feed and tend; this is my body, for you, my foster-father, to support and protect. He wore it in its state of maturity, espoused to poverty and hardship for our sakes;... This is my body, life-giving and life-bringing, stinted of food and sleep, travelling mile upon mile over weary roads, to claim that Church which is my destined bride. He wore it in its state of death, drained of sweat and blood for our sakes;... This is my body, so torn with scourges and buffeting that it can scarcely be recognized; for you, with the nails, to crucify; for you, with the spear, to pierce; for you, Joseph, to bury; for you, Magdalen, to embalm. *Hoc est corpus meum*, the body of a man, belonging to me, who am God; here it is, helpless; here it is, overspent; here it is, pale in death.

And in the greatest, the most wonderful of all his sacraments, once again we remind ourselves, "No sacrifice, no offering was thy demand; thou hast endowed me with a body instead." Only this time it is not our body, but his. In that daily miracle of his love, he wants to give us grace for the soul's needs, as in the hour of birth, or of marriage, or of death; but this time it is he who says, *Hoc est corpus meum*, and, so saying, he shows himself again in those three states of his Incarnation. Every communion we make is a birth, a marriage, and a death. As those words are pronounced, he comes silently into the priest's hands, as he came to Bethlehem; "he shall come down like rain into a fleece of wool," the Psalm tells us (72:6); so he came, and so he comes. When last you went to communion, what were the dispositions of your heart as the bell tinkled in the sanctuary? Were you waiting for him, like the shepherds of Bethlehem; were you keeping watch, as they were, keeping watch over your thoughts, as they over their flocks, so that you were ready for his coming? Or was your heart like the wayside inn, too full of other guests to give a thought to his miraculous birth? When we make our preparation for communion, there should be a silence as of midnight in our hearts; not a feverish activity of aspirations and petitions, but an interior silence that banishes from the mind the busy echoes of its daily preoccupations; those plans we were forming, those grudges we were nursing, those anxieties we were harbouring, those fears we were encouraging—well, perhaps it is too much to ask that we should banish them altogether, but they should be hushed, as men's footsteps are hushed outside the door of a sick-room. It is in the silence of the heart that we shall hear that whisper, *Hoc est corpus meum*, and know that Christ is born.

But if our Lord's presence in the Holy Eucharist means a birth, it also means a marriage; the moment at which we receive the Blessed Sacrament is the moment at which he plights his love to us in a supreme manner, making us one with himself. *Hoc est corpus meum*—it is the voice of the bridegroom in the Canticles, standing behind the wall, and bidding his beloved come away into the fields

Sacrament Most Holy

and the villages, rousing us from the heavy sleep of our neglect. When we receive holy communion, it is well enough if we find ourselves in the dispositions of Martha, eagerly entertaining our divine guest with prayers for this and that; for the graces we covet, strength to resist temptations, the needs of the Church or of our friends. But, just at that moment, it is surely better still if we find ourselves in the dispositions of Mary Magdalen, sitting at his feet and hearing his word; sitting at his feet, in a humility which makes us forget self, hearing his word, in a raptness of attention which makes us forget all besides. Just in that moment, we want to be all for him, *dilectus meus mihi, et ego illi*; that is the good part, surely, which shall not be taken away from us.

And finally, our Lord's presence in the Holy Eucharist means a death. Not only in the sense that somehow, mysteriously, he who was immolated once for all on Calvary makes fresh offering of his death every time we celebrate the holy mysteries; but in this sense too, that his sacramental presence in our bodies at least is a transitory one; it is withdrawn from us when he has given us the opportunity to profit by it as we should. And at our Lord's tomb, as at our Lord's cradle, there were two classes of watchers. The soldiers had been set there to watch, and they fell asleep. While they slept, Mary Magdalen and the other holy women were on their way to embalm the body with spices. And when our mortal bodies share the privilege of the holy sepulchre, to receive into them the body of Christ, which are we more like—the soldiers who went to sleep, or the women who could not rest till they had embalmed his memory? When we make our thanksgiving after communion, we ought to hoard up those precious moments as if they were some precious liquid, ointment of right spikenard, that we must guard jealously even as we run, for fear that a drop of them should be wasted. Ten minutes, it may be, is all we can spare when Mass is ended, but those ten minutes, if they are well used, will suffice to grant us the privilege Mary Magdalen had, of hearing him call us by our own name, of calling him by his.

This is my body, born for you at Bethlehem, and between the priest's hands. This is my body, spent with labours for my bride the Church, made one with my faithful in this sacrament. This is my body, forgotten and remembered in death, forgotten or remembered, every day, by the souls it has visited and nourished.

X

The Best Man

He must become more and more, I must become less and less.
(John 3:30)

I think I am right in saying that the feast of Corpus Christi falls, this year, on the latest date at which it can possibly fall, the 24th of June. And, so falling, by a curious coincidence, it clashes with, and supersedes, the only very great feast which Corpus Christi ever does supersede—the Nativity of St John the Baptist. To be sure, we do not let him fall out of the calendar altogether; we celebrate him tomorrow. But, for once, the great forerunner comes lagging behind his Master.

I do not think there is any saint you can imagine accepting that situation with a better grace than St John the Baptist. He was born, if we may dare to say so, to be the odd man out. Our Lord himself tells us that. Poor John, he says, the greatest man ever born of woman, and yet he is less than the least of you people here, because the kingdom of heaven is for you, not for him. He takes rank with the heroes of the Old Testament, who lived in hope and never saw their hopes realized; prophets and kings desired it long, and died before the sight. Everybody is rushing the barriers, Tom, Dick, and Harry swarming into the kingdom of heaven, the violent take it by force, and he, John, is left outside. Remember, St John wasn't dead when our Lord said that; he was only in prison. But St John was not destined, that is the point, to see the world's salvation achieved. And St John realized that, felt that. The crowds which used to come and demand baptism from him had thinned down into a mere trickle; and his disciples complained that this new prophet, Jesus of Nazareth, had stolen his thunder, had borrowed his methods, and was eclipsing him. And St John replied in the words I quoted to you just now, "He must become more and more; I must become less and less." It was his fate, he said, to be like the best man at the wedding; all the interest centred in another, all the acclamations reserved for another; and he must stand by—jealous? Out of humour? No, "rejoicing at hearing the bridegroom's voice." He had learned the trick of standing on one side, and making way for Jesus Christ.

That is why, today, I am proposing St John to you as one of the saints of the Blessed Sacrament. He never lived to kneel at the Last Supper and receive the body of Christ from the hands of Christ himself. He never lived to wait with our Lady and the apostles, and see the Holy Spirit which descended upon Christ at the Jordan descend upon Christ's Church in the cenacle. But he has left us one golden phrase, which should never be far from our minds when we are waiting for our blessed Lord to come to us in holy communion; "he must become more and more; I must become less and less."

If you look at the last verse of the first chapter of St Luke, you will find the words, "the child grew"; that refers to St John. If you look a little lower down, in the fortieth verse of the next chapter, you will find the same words again, "the child grew"; this time, they refer to our Lord. Take those two verses together, and you have the

Sacrament Most Holy

whole biography of St John. Outwardly, St John grew up; inwardly, in his soul, he never grew up—it was the Christ-child, his cousin, that grew up within him. "Some fell upon good ground, and these sprouted and grew, and yielded a harvest"—there, in the parable of the sower, you have the explanation. The sower sows the word, and the word of God, we are told, came upon John in the wilderness. The word of God, the grain of wheat which falls into the ground and dies, that it may bring forth much fruit, was sown in the heart of St John; and what grew up was not St John; it was the word of God, Jesus Christ.

The seed sown, what a splendid parable that is of the influence of divine grace in human hearts, and how unsparingly the New Testament makes use of it! Go out into the country at this time of year, and look at some piece of ground that has only been recently reclaimed for tillage, in these days when every acre is of value. What do you find there? A sea of green; catching the eye, as the sea does, with its waves of light and shadow, when the breeze goes rippling over its surface. But it is all one uniform surface; nothing, you would say, but green blades everywhere, each bowed by the growing burden of the ear that is forming on it. Then, go up closer and look down underneath the crop. What do you find now? Nettles, thistles, docks, bracken, brambles, ragged robin, willow-herb, a network of wild undergrowth. These were the native masters of the soil, till the farmer, the other day, buried in it this mysterious treasure of good grain. It has been a struggle for domination, it is a struggle still, between those old, rugged native growths, and the patient intruder. A struggle, which of them shall enjoy the richness of the soil beneath; a struggle, which of them shall grow higher and shut out the sun's light from the other. And the crop which man intruded there has won.

That is an image of your soul and mine. Or rather, would God that it were! It is the image of a soul in which divine grace has the upper hand; the soul of a saint, or something next door to a saint. The Psalmist represents almighty God as saying to our Lord, *Dominare in medio inimicorum tuorum,* "Dominate amongst thy enemies" (Ps. 109:2). And that should be our prayer, every time our Lord comes to us in holy communion; we want him to dominate in our souls, in the midst of his enemies—our souls are so full of his enemies, pride, covetousness, resentment, self-indulgence, ready to dispute every inch of territory with him. We are fallen creatures; thorns and briers spring up not only in the ground which was cursed for our sakes, but in the fertile depths of our own souls, of which it is the image. Grace comes as an intruder, to struggle for the mastery in hostile surroundings. And the most sanctified of human souls is no better than that cornfield we were considering just now; look under the surface, and all the human passions are still there underneath, got down but not fully eradicated. God help us, what of your soul and mine?

He must become more and more, I must become less and less. Rooted deep in our nature, mysteriously prolific, spreading out in a network of subtle ramifications, lies the instinct of self-assertion. You see it in its crudest form in children, that desire to show off, to be thought important, which is sometimes so irritating, sometimes so amusing. School-days come, and school-masters combine with school-friends to weed out this obvious defect. But they haven't really weeded it out, they've only driven it underground. It is rooted

Sacrament Most Holy

in us none the less firmly—perhaps we ought to say, all the more firmly—because we are compelled by the conventions of society to cover it up and pretend it is not there. But we know that it is there; how few people there are that can take it well, even outwardly, when their advice is not asked for, or is asked for and not taken; when they are passed over in the filling up of a vacancy and somebody else is put in instead; when some professional rival achieves fame, in the very department where they hoped to achieve fame themselves! Even outwardly; and when we come to look inside, each of us into his own heart, how much deeper it lies, often, than the world knows, that bitter feeling of ill-usage we have when our self-importance is wounded! Don't let's be too despondent about it, if we find such feelings are often with us; they are common enough, God knows, in the life of any moderately good Christian. But they are perhaps the surest sign which could be given us, that we are not saints.

And one of the reasons, surely, why our Lord comes to us in holy communion is to make us more Christ-assertive, and therefore less self-assertive, as life goes on. The two qualities, you see, cannot really exist together; or perhaps we ought to say that they can exist together, but they cannot flourish side by side. In your corn-field, the bracken will win here, the wheat there, but one will always get the better of the other. So it is with us; he must become more and more, I must become less and less; you can be sure that Christ is not yet dominating among his enemies, if that instinct of self-assertiveness is still strong. That "I" which is so covetous of petty superiorities; that "I" which infects even our prayer, even our virtues, making us want to be pure so that we may feel pure, be humble so that we may be free to criticize the pride of others, be mortified so that we can congratulate ourselves on being mortified, instead of simply wanting God's will to be done in us, and in everybody else. The "I" which takes all its losses and disappointments so badly, asking why *this* should have passed others by, and have been reserved for *me*.

Shall we try to humble ourselves occasionally, get some idea of the little progress *we* have made, by thinking about today's saint, St John the Baptist? When the priest holds up the sacred Host before giving us communion, it is from St John the Baptist that he quotes. "Look, this is the Lamb of God; this is he who takes away the sins of the world!" (John 1:29). And when St John said that, he knew that he was directing the attention of his disciples towards another Teacher; that he would lose them, that he would lose, gradually, all his popularity, all his chance of getting a hearing, as the result of this competition; and he didn't mind. Shut out from the kingdom of heaven, like a child flattening its nose against a shop-window when it has no money to buy the coveted things that are set out there; and he didn't mind. He must become more and more, I must become less and less; less of me, so that there may be more of him.

Do we sometimes find it difficult to stir our imaginations with the thought of holy men who died long ago? Then let me, for a moment, evoke a more recent memory. Some of you will have known, most of you will have heard—he has often stood in this pulpit—the great Dominican whom death has just removed from us, Father Vincent McNabb. When he delivered his memorable panegyric on Father Bede Jarrett, he took a text which refers to St John the Baptist, "He was a burning and a shining light" (John 5:35). Let me suggest to you this for *his* epitaph, "He must become more and more, I must become less and less." Here was a man whose very eccentricities were due to his absorption in the Christ he preached. People often felt inclined to say to him, "You are forgetting yourself, Father"; and they would have been right—he always did forget himself. His was a voice crying in the wilderness, crying out, in Hyde Park, to a London which would not listen; in these last few weeks, through his mortal ailment, that voice became a whisper, scarcely audible, but he went on. He must become less and less; but we knew that Christ was becoming more and more in him, all through those last heroic days. May his soul find, beyond the grave, the rest it never asked for here; may his gracious influence still haunt, in the troubled times that are coming, his familiar walks, the streets he knew and the city he loved so well.

XI

Self-Examination

*My judgment is judgment indeed; it is not I alone,
my Father who sent me is with me.* (JOHN 8:16)

IT IS ALWAYS INTERESTING to speculate what historians will be saying, a hundred years hence, about the period in which you are living. What will they be saying about us, what figure shall we cut in the estimation of posterity, living in this uneasy twilight of 1946, an uncertain twilight, whether of dusk or dawn? One thing they will say, I fancy, of which for the most part we are quite unconscious. This will be regarded as the age of the great judicial trials. On a scale unexampled in history, judgment is being passed on men who, till yesterday, felt that they were above the law; felt, too often, that considerations of human justice need not apply to their actions. Today, their lives are in jeopardy, all over the continent of Europe, and in the remote islands of the eastern sea.

It would be an excess of charity to pretend that all these legal proceedings, everywhere, are being conducted with legal fairness. The consciences of English people are only committed to seeing justice done in a limited number of them. And I think we can derive

---

This sermon was preached at the time of the Nuremberg trials.

great comfort from the criticisms which foolish people are making, in the newspapers especially, about the slowness and elaborateness of the procedure on which we, more than any other nation in the world, obstinately insist. It is easy for the cynic to point out that in spite of it all we shall probably be accused, in a hundred years' time, of having taken vengeance on our enemies with a hypocritical show of impartiality. It is easy to object that there is no instance in history where a man tried by his enemies has had, indisputably, a fair trial. We can afford to neglect such criticisms. We are not concerned to put ourselves right in the eyes of posterity. We are concerned, when we pass judgment on our fellow creatures, to put ourselves right in the eyes of almighty God.

When we judge, remember, we are usurping the privilege of God himself. When we judge our enemies, how shall we make certain that we are not blinded by prejudice? The evidence cannot be too laboriously compiled, the pleadings cannot be examined too scrupulously here. The man who judges a fellow creature on earth stands his own trial, in doing so, before the tribunal of eternal justice; not less so the nation which judges the crimes of another nation. We, as we give just or unjust verdict, as we impose deserved or undeserved sentence, at this hour, are claiming for ourselves, or forfeiting, the divine approval.

It was this contrast between human justice and divine to which our Lord was drawing attention when he used the words from which I have taken my text. "You," he says to the Jews, "set yourselves up to judge after your earthly fashion; I do not set myself up to judge anybody. And what if I should judge? My judgment is judgment indeed; it is not I alone, my Father who sent me is with me"

RONALD KNOX

(John 6:15-16). The opinions which his contemporaries formed about Jesus of Nazareth were utterly worthless; dictated to them by prejudice, by injured vanity, by jealous hatred of a life spent in doing good. The opinions which Jesus of Nazareth formed about his contemporaries were so many decrees registered in eternity. The Father was with him; he saw with the eyes of that infallible wisdom. The Father was with him; he made allowances with the clemency of that inexhaustible love. The Father was with him; he pronounced sentence with all the terrors of that irresistible power. Every perspective seen by the eyes of the Incarnate was true; he was himself the truth.

Why does he say, "I do not set myself up to judge anybody"? Is not this the same Jesus of Nazareth, who promised that he would come again to judge the living and the dead? Yes, but he was not judging them yet. You see, it was not necessary. He has only to come and live amongst us men, and we men, at the mere neighbourhood of him, pass judgment on ourselves. We accept or reject him, and thereby betray ourselves as the kind of men we are; no more is needed for our condemnation or acquittal. That is, in a sense, the whole message of St John's Gospel. "Rejection," he says, "lies in this, that when the light came into the world men preferred darkness to light; preferred it, because their doings were evil." All those dark secrets of the human conscience, on which our limited human knowledge finds it so difficult to pass judgment, gave themselves away when the light came into the world; it is an automatic process, the dispelling of darkness by light. And our Lord could tell us quite truly, that he had come to save the world, not to pass sentence on it. But the people who rejected him thereby passed sentence on themselves.

Sacrament Most Holy

After all, you see, when we talk about having to undergo judgment when we are dead, we are only using a kind of metaphor, a kind of analogy. God's judgments are not like ours; he does not have to find out the truth, he knows it already. There is no citing of witnesses, no discussion of arguments for and against; when we die, we are judged already—our own lives, our own dispositions, mark us down already for the doom that is to be ours in eternity. When man judges man, the accused knows whether he is innocent or guilty; it is for the judge to find out. When God judges man, the judge knows the truth already; it is the accused that has to learn it. Our judgment will be the exhibition to ourselves, and later to humanity at large, of our own record; in the sight of God, that record is already plain to view.

We are often encouraged to think seriously about the hour of death, and to remind ourselves that our judgment will immediately follow it. That is, no doubt, a salutary exercise of piety, but familiarity has staled it for us, and we sometimes find that it does not affect our lives as it ought to. We think of our lives as a record folded over and put into an envelope and pigeon-holed somewhere in a kind of celestial clearing office, where they will lie, till the moment of our death, unread. Then, to be sure, the envelope will be opened, and eternal justice will take a look at its contents. But by then, so much may have happened; that pious old age we look forward to, that edifying death-bed! It seems such a long distance away. I wonder if we shouldn't do well sometimes to remember that, in a sense, our judgment is happening *now*. You are wondering whether you will or will not decide to go to confession, and renounce, in your act of contrition, some darling sin. And God is already sitting in judgment on you; picture, if you will, the black cap as lying on the desk in front of him. Picture him as saying, "This shall be the test. If this creature of mine cannot do so much for me, this very little I ask of him, then he is no use; nothing can ever be made of him, nothing will ever pierce that conscience of his, it is hardened beyond remedy." The judgment is set, and the books are opened; I am calling down upon myself, here and now, a verdict which will take its effect in eternity.

"What a curious sermon," you are saying, "for Corpus Christi Day! We might have been given something less depressing to think about, on this day of all days, than death and judgment." Yes, but I can't help it; it's in this morning's epistle; it's all over this morning's epistle. "It is the Lord's death you are heralding, whenever you eat this bread and drink this cup, until he comes; and therefore, if anyone eats this bread or drinks this cup of the Lord unworthily, he will be held to account for the Lord's body and blood. A man must examine himself first, and then eat of that bread and drink of that cup; he is eating and drinking damnation to himself if he eats and drinks unworthily, not recognizing the Lord's body for what it is" (1 Cor. 11:27–29). The Christian who partakes of this gift without concerning himself to ask whether he is in a fit state to receive it becomes the accomplice of Pontius Pilate, judging and misjudging Christ. By not recognizing that virgin-born body for what it is, he associates himself with the crime which crucified it. Whatever else the Church wants us to have in mind when we keep the Corpus Christi feast, it is certain that she means us to spare a thought for the dangers of sacrilegious communion. She comes back to the subject again, you see, in the *Lauda Sion*:

Sacrament Most Holy

> The good, the guilty share therein,
> With sure increase of grace or sin,
> The ghostly life, or ghostly death:

she wants us to be quite certain where we stand. And we stand in the dock.

Our blessed Lord, in his divine nature, is present to us at all times, is close to us at all times. Yet, to allow for the weakness of our own imaginations, he likes us to think of him, doesn't he, as coming to pay us a visit now and again. "My Father and I will come to him" (John 14:23), he says; and again, comparing himself still more vividly to some earthly guest, "Behold, I stand at the door and knock" (Apoc. 3:20). It is our fault, remember, if that visit proves to be a surprise visit. He does not come to us in the manner of a suspicious policeman, or a prying schoolmaster, to see what we are up to. No, he who came into the world to save it, not to pass sentence on it, comes to us still not to find out what is wrong with us, but eager for our good. Only, when he comes and knocks at the door, if that knock is followed by scuffling, and silence, and the door does not open, it means that all is not well within. We were not ready for him; we were taken off our guard. And, found in that posture, we have proclaimed ourselves guilty men. It is not he, it is we ourselves, that have passed the sentence of our condemnation.

As the rays of the sun, whose heat is present everywhere, are caught and focused in a single point by the lens of a burning-glass, so our Lord will have these celestial visitations of his focused for us, crystallized and concentrated for us under the forms of outward things, when he comes to us through his sacred humanity in the

RONALD KNOX

Holy Eucharist. Here at least we cannot complain that he takes us by surprise. He is so utterly condescending, in this sacrament of his humiliation, that he will visit us at a time of our own choosing, will leave it to us to invite him when we want him to come. His knock at the door shall be gentler than ever; there can be no excuse, surely, for haste or confusion within. And yet…is it always so? We so easily get wrapped up in our own petty concerns, get carried away by our own foolish trains of thought, that most of us know what it is to hear the bell ring at the *Domine non sum dignus*, and be awoken from our daydreams by the sudden intrusion of that supreme reality.

That only happens at the surface level of consciousness. We ought not, I think, to worry about it a great deal when we find ourselves, day after day or week after week, incapable (I don't think that is putting it too strongly) of concentrating our thoughts on what we are doing when we go to communion until the very last moment. This habit of woolgathering is a weakness in us, not a crime; and it is certainly wrong to argue, "It seems impossible for me to receive holy communion with anything like recollectedness, therefore I shall go to communion less often." We shall do far better to communicate often, and to go on apologizing to our Lord for this persistent absent-mindedness of ours, which is so far from representing our real attitude. No, what St Paul wants us to be careful about is something different; "a man must examine himself first"— we have got to dig down below that surface level, and lay bare our secret infidelities. Those grudges against our neighbour which we forget all the time, but forget about them because they are buried so deep; those obstinate attachments to deliberate venial sin, perhaps

Sacrament Most Holy

only needing opportunity, perhaps only needing more enterprise, to turn them into something worse—those are the real marks of disrespect we show when our Lord comes to visit us. And we shall continue to show those marks of disrespect, until we learn to do what St Paul tells us we ought to be doing all the time, examine ourselves. Oh, we do that, every now and again, when we go to confession; but do we really dig deep enough? The gracious influence which comes to us in the Holy Eucharist ought to fill the soul to its depths. But, at those depths, it encounters infidelities, reluctances, a half-hearted attitude towards eternity; an unspiritual habit of mind, which challenges and resists it.

We have to welcome our Lord in holy communion, not only as the friend who comes to visit us, not only as the physician who comes to heal us, but as the auditor (if I may put it as prosaically as that) who comes to put our accounts straight for us. How wonderful if the first voice which greets us after death should be heard saying, "His sins? That is all right; we have been into all that before!"

XII

The Thing That Matters

*It is through him, then, that we must offer to God
a continual sacrifice of praise.* (HEB. 13:15)

I WAS PREACHING LAST SUNDAY down at Exeter, to commemorate a sad and much-forgotten event in English history. Four hundred years ago an order went out from the Government in London that the Latin Mass should be discontinued, and a new, English service-book should be used in all churches and chapels of the realm. It was the signal for a rising among the men of the Western counties, who took up arms in defence of the old religion; and the Government had to call in German and Italian mercenaries before the rebellion was stamped out in blood.

Not for the first time I found myself wondering why it was that this particular piece of provocation, the English service-book, should have been the signal for an outbreak. After all, the people of England had put up with a good deal already. The rights of the Holy See had been repudiated, and for fifteen years the whole country had been in schism. The monasteries, so intimately bound up with the religious life of the Middle Ages, had been dissolved and lay in ruins. Gangs of hooligans, with royal encouragement, went about everywhere breaking down the statues of our Lady and the saints,

Sacrament Most Holy

defacing even the pictures in our churches. But when all that had been done, one line still remained which you must not overstep, on pain of driving the common folk into violent insurrection; you must not touch the Mass.

It was not open provocation, only the thin end of the wedge, in 1549. The new service-book, modelled much more closely on our Catholic liturgy than anything the Church of England has had since, was perhaps meant to be a compromise; more probably, to be a first instalment of change. The communion service, "commonly called the Mass," had a recognizable Canon, offered prayer for the dead, commemorated our blessed Lady and the saints. But already the men of the West saw what was coming, and turned out with the rude armour of country folk crying, "We will not receive the new service, because it is but like a Christmas game." There was plenty of fine English prose about it, but it lacked reality. It was not the Mass.

In a curious way, when they made that protest, the insurgents defined an issue, marked out an arena of conflict, for three centuries ahead. Within a lifetime, the word "Mass" came to have an abominable sound in English ears; it belonged to the jargon of a discredited underworld. To say Mass became high treason; if you described a person as going to Mass, you meant that he was a Popish recusant. And the stigma has persisted right up to our own times; at the beginning of this century, an epigrammatic statesman could still arouse prejudice against us by declaring, "It is the Mass that matters." And we caught up the slogan, and made it our own; it is the Mass that matters, that is what we *must* get people to understand.

What was clear, I think, to the men of the West country, was that the Government wanted to abolish the Holy Eucharist as a sacrifice, while retaining holy communion as one of the sacraments. And they demanded roundly that Mass should be said "without any persons communicating with the priest." I'm afraid we have to admit it, our forefathers in the later Middle Ages did not use the sacraments as faithfully as they might have done, as they should have done; a bad tradition had grown up. That was why the Council of Trent expressed a wish that "at each Mass the faithful who are present should communicate"; for all the world as if they shared the opinions of the Reformers. But the emphasis was entirely different. The Fathers of Trent were determined to honour the sacrament of holy communion; the Reformers were concerned to discredit the doctrine of the eucharistic sacrifice. They weren't hardy enough to deny it, but they meant to obscure it, to soft-pedal it, until gradually it fell into oblivion.

The men who died at Exeter in 1549 saw through that intention of the Government, and were determined to force the issue. They had grown up in an England where Christ was offered day by day at a thousand altars for the living and the dead; this new England, in which the Lord's Supper would be administered once a week if there was enough demand for it among the parishioners, was something they had no use for. And that remained, as I say, for three centuries the whole pattern of English religion; on one side there were the old-fashioned people, a majority at first, then a dwindling minority, who held by the Mass; on the other side a confused body of Anglicans and sectaries who sang psalms, listened to sermons, and every now and then, if they were pious folk and were feeling pious, partook of the Lord's Supper.

Have I spoilt the feast for you by talking so much about history,

Sacrament Most Holy

, y by recalling "old, unhappy, far-off things and battles of long ago"? Forgive me, but I think we do well to remember these lost causes of a bygone age, if only so as to remind ourselves of the eternal thing they stood for. I do not mean, heaven forbid, that you and I should bear a grudge against our non-Catholic neighbours, as if they were responsible for the loss sustained by English religion four centuries back. No, but the truth ever shines brighter by contrast, and we shall understand our own faith better if we understand the meaning, however dimly realized, that underlay the protest of the West country people so long ago. We shall see the doctrine of the Holy Mass as a thing worth living for, if we can see why it was, in their day, a thing worth dying for.

What is it exactly that the old-fashioned Protestant misses as he kneels at the communion-rails? To be sure, he finds there nothing of the miraculous; he has lost sight of what is our chief motive for admiration and gratitude; if the doctrine of transubstantiation is proposed to him, he dismisses it at once as a piece of medieval superstition. His theology, then, is hopelessly attenuated, but I am not thinking so much about theology, just now. I am thinking of his devotional attitude; and his devotional attitude is not, perhaps, so unlike ours as this theology would lead you to expect. He does, after all, hope to receive supernatural grace. The reception of it, he would tell you, depends entirely on the faith which he brings to the exercise; if faith were lacking, he would receive nothing, because there would be nothing to receive. Once more, he is wrong; but since he does in fact approach in a spirit of faith, the embarrassment does not arise. He hopes to receive sacramental grace, and there is something more; he probably believes that our Lord is present in a special way, communicating himself mysteriously to the soul of the worshipper. About the manner of that presence he can tell you nothing; he avoids the question, and, if you press him, takes refuge in metaphors. But, left to himself, he approaches with awe, none the less real, none the less comforting, because the object of it remains undefined. "Christ's was the word that spake it; he took the bread and brake it, and what his word doth make it, that I believe and take it"—the lines are attributed to Queen Elizabeth, and if she was really the author of them, I think most of us will be inclined to blame her for shirking an issue which it was her duty to face. But if they are quoted by somebody born outside the Church, somebody who has no head for theology, I do not know why such a person may not have made, according to his lights, a good spiritual communion.

His devotional life is impoverished, rather, for *this* reason—that his communion service has nothing of Mass about it. It has been a mere service of consecration, in which lifeless things were set apart to be the pledge of *his* salvation, to bring a special grace to *his* soul. As water in baptism, so here bread and wine, were hallowed only for the satisfaction of a human need; Christ became present, in whatever sense Christ did become present, only so as to be made one with him. There was no transaction external to himself, in which and for the purpose of which Christ would have become present, even if there had been nobody to communicate. There was no sacrifice.

We of the old faith, instinctively, approach the mystery of Holy Eucharist from the other end. For us, holy communion, important as it is, awe-inspiring as it is, figures as something secondary in

Sacrament Most Holy

intention to the Mass itself; a gracious corollary, a stupendous after-effect, which unites us in a special way with the thing done. For us the immediate, dazzling truth is that here and all over the world Christ, in the person of the priest, is offering Christ under the forms of bread and wine in perfect sacrifice to the eternal Father. If I am worthy, if I am willing, he gives himself to me; but, worthy or no, willing or no, he gives himself for me, as for all mankind, his brothers; on earth, as in heaven, he is our High Priest and representative. All that vision, familiar to the Middle Ages, faded from the eyes of English folk when German and Italian troops raised the siege of Exeter.

I have used the word "impoverishment"; when they abolished the Mass, the Government of that day robbed the English people no less really, and far more importantly, than when they took away the common lands which had been free to all in the time of the monasteries. The thoughts of the Christian were turned fatally in upon himself: "What effect is this sacrament going to produce in me? How am I to get rid of my sins? How can I be certain that I am, here and now, in the grace of Christ? Can I feel his love, here and now, at work in me? Am I predestined to a happy eternity?"—and so on. And the result of that was scruples, and religious melancholy, and despair, and a reaction which made men turn away from the whole Christian idea. You see, a man who enjoys bodily health is not always thinking about whether he is well or not, and a Christian who enjoys spiritual health is not always thinking about whether he is saved or not. I don't mean that he doesn't want to be saved, I don't mean that he is prepared to neglect his salvation; but his first concern is not that, it is something other. His first concern is that God

85

should be worthily worshipped, for the sake of his own glory. And we Catholics have the assurance that that is being done, whenever we go into a church and find a priest saying Mass. The priest may be somebody for whom we have little respect, somebody who does not strike us as an exact follower of his Master's rule; God forgive us, how few of us priests are anything like that! No, but he is a priest, and in him we see the hand of Christ invisibly extended; Christ is here, offering himself to the Father, and through him not you or I but all mankind is pouring out its helpless, stammering accents of worship. God's glory first, the Paternoster said, and the Victim broken; and *then* we can gather round the altar rails, and make the sacrifice, by communicating with it, more than ever our own.

It's the Mass that matters. No need to follow the theologians into their nice disquisitions about the exact meaning of sacrifice, the exact sense in which the Mass is a sacrifice, the exact moment at which the sacrifice takes place. All *that* we can take as read; enough that the Catholic religion points us to an altar and bids us fall down in worship. To us, and to our brethren still separated from us, may God restore his ancient mercies; now, when so many other lights are put out, may England, as in happier days, bear integral witness to his truth.

XIII

Real Bread

Who will come and get him food, no price to be paid? (Isa. 55:1)

There is a curious point about our Lord's teaching, or at any rate about that more intimate, more characteristic teaching preserved for us in the Gospel of St John, which we sometimes fail to notice because we are so accustomed, nowadays, to the use of metaphor in common speech. I mean this point—that our Lord does not simply compare heavenly things with earthly by way of illustration, does not simply say, for example, "You see that vine? Well, that vine will give you some idea of the unity of the Church." Rather, he treats all the earthly things with which we are familiar in this world of sense as if they were mere shadows, mere inferior copies of the reality which awaits us in heaven. He starts, if we may say so, at the other end; not at the earthly end which is more familiar to us ordinary human beings, but at the heavenly end which is more familiar to the incarnate Son of God.

So it is when he talks to the Samaritan woman; "If thou knewest what it is God gives, and who it is that is saying to thee, Give me drink, it would have been for thee to ask him instead, and he would have given thee living water" (John 4:10). By "living water" he does not mean fresh water or running water, as the woman supposes. He means that all the water you can find in this world of sense, the purest, the freshest to be had anywhere, is only dead water; the real water, the real living water, is something which does not belong to the world of sense at all. We shall never know what water really means until we have the direct experience of that reality of grace of which water is only a pale image. So with the vine; the vines you may see growing on some hillside in France are not real vines, he tells us, they are only a sort of imitation. We shall never understand the mystery of organic growth, of that principle in nature whereby a tree or a plant goes on producing fresh shoots according to its kind, until we know, as not even the saints can know it on earth, the nature of that bond which unites all Christian people with their divine Head, and through him with one another.

And so it is, he tells us, with the very bread we eat; the simplest, most primitive fact of human life—so much so that the old poets used to describe the human race as "men that live by bread." The true bread, the living bread, is not the common bread which we eat. The common bread which we eat is only a sham, a copy, an image of that true bread which came down from heaven. And if we ask what is the true bread which came down from heaven, he has given us the answer: "I myself am the living bread; the man who eats my flesh and drinks my blood enjoys eternal life" (John 6:55). You see, we are so materialistic, our minds are so chained to the things of sense, that we imagine our Lord as instituting the Blessed Sacrament with bread and wine as the remote matter of it because bread and wine reminded him of that grace which he intended the Blessed Sacrament to bestow. But, if you come to think of it,

Sacrament Most Holy

it was just the other way about. When he created the world, he gave common bread and wine for our use in order that we might understand what the Blessed Sacrament was when it came to be instituted. He did not design the sacred Host to be something like bread. He designed bread to be something like the sacred Host.

Always, it is the things which affect us outwardly and impress themselves on our senses that are the shams, the imaginaries; reality belongs to the things of the spirit. All the din and clatter of the streets, all the great factories which dominate our landscape, are only echoes and shadows if you think of them for a moment in the light of eternity; the reality is in here, is there above the altar, is that part of it which our eyes cannot see and our senses cannot distinguish. The motto on Cardinal Newman's tomb ought to be the funeral motto of every Catholic, *Ex umbris et imaginibus in veritatem*—Out of shadows and appearances into the truth. When death brings us into another world, the experience will not be that of one who falls asleep and dreams, but that of one who wakes from a dream into the full light of day. Here, we are so surrounded by the things of sense that we take them for the full reality. Only sometimes we have a glimpse which corrects that wrong perspective. And above all, when we see the Blessed Sacrament enthroned, we should look up towards that white disc which shines in the monstrance as towards a chink through which, just for a moment, the light of the other world shines through.

There are periods, there are moments in history, which seem to men living at the time to show up the world for the transient, fleeting thing it is. Wars or famines or pestilence have depopulated countries, and have left the survivors uncertain of their prospects, uncertain of life itself; the energies of human nature seem to have used themselves up, and it feels as if the forces of inanimate nature, too, were threatened with dissolution. At such times, men have often turned to their religion with more ardour, have separated themselves from the world and gone to live as hermits or in the cloister, reminded at last that we have here no abiding city. You will catch the echoes of that feeling in the sermons of St Gregory in the sixth century, in the rhythm of Bernard of Morlaix in the twelfth. It is not an illusion people get at such times that the world is transitory. Rather at such times they lose the illusion that the world is permanent. They realize more than at other times what is true at all times, that the whole of this visible creation is but a thin plank between us and eternity.

Now here is an extraordinary thing—that *we* live in times when, perhaps more than ever before, we ought to see through the hollowness of the material things around us, and yet, so far have we travelled from the age of faith, we love the things of the world more than ever, clasp them more than ever, as we see them ready to disappear from us. Anybody who knows anything knows that our country is in a bad way, and that other countries, when you come to look at them, are not much better off than ourselves. Unemployment is the difficulty which most readily leaps to the eye, but unemployment is only a symptom of some hidden and mysterious disease which has come upon an over-civilized world. A trade depression, we say, a slump in the world market; but does anybody really know what is happening? Does anybody really know how soon we may be involved in the miseries of wholesale bankruptcy? Our comfortable world of prosperity, inherited from our Victorian

Sacrament Most Holy

ancestors, is threatening to tumble about our ears; and we smile nervously and hope for the best.

And here is what makes it still more extraordinary—we do not owe our present troubles to any of the common forces of nature, to a world-wide drought, to torrential rains, to any pestilence among mankind or blight among the crops. Something that is happening in the unreal world of high finance is having its effects, devastating effects, upon the real world—or so we think it—in which men must earn their bread or starve if they cannot come by it. Imagine some visitant from the past who should come to earth nowadays and hear of our modern distresses. So much poverty, he would say, so much uncertainty about the very means of livelihood—I suppose you must have had bad harvests, and there is not enough corn to go round? And we should have to tell him that it is just the opposite; that whole stocks of grain are being destroyed for fear that corn should be too plentiful, and therefore too cheap! You see, we are caught up in the wheels of our own economic system. The fields of wheat flourish, there is corn and wine and oil in abundance, there is treasure still locked in the bosom of earth; and yet through our own laws of supply and demand, laws which have no root in nature, but depend simply upon our human actions, the whole world is at a standstill! Did we not say well that this world in which we live is a world of shadows? When forces that have no existence outside our own wills can threaten society with destruction?

And the effect of all that on us? Is it to drive us nearer to God, to make us disgusted with the insufficiency of this world? I am afraid it is very difficult to avoid the impression that it is all the other way; that we try to forget our solicitudes by drowning ourselves in

RONALD KNOX

pleasures and amusements, by getting all that we can out of today, when tomorrow has so little to offer. If the investments that call for our savings are insecure, very well, we will not save; if hard work earns so little, we will give up to leisure the hours that were meant for work. That is not the moral God means us to draw. He means us to realize, when our labour is ill-paid, that all labour is ill-paid which is crowned with earthly rewards; he means us to understand, when money is hard to come by and hard to keep, that all treasure is wasted when it is laid up on earth. Do not labour for the meat which perishes, he tells us; lay up for yourselves treasure in heaven.

Without money and without price.... Lord, give us always this bread. That is his invitation; that should be our response. His temporal gifts he will lavish at one time, withhold from us at another; that is because they do not really matter; they only refer to the needs of this life, such a short one. Your fathers, he says to the Jews, did eat manna and are dead; more highly privileged, you would think, than any nation on the earth, they were kept alive from day to day with supplies of food miraculously maintained and miraculously multiplied. And the upshot of it? They went the way of all flesh at last; they passed over the horizon, and the slopes of the wilderness grew white with manna no more. Does he not, perhaps, say the same to us? Your fathers did eat manna and are dead; in the times of national prosperity, I gave them such abundance as no other nation has known; their fleets peopled the seas, their workshops rang with industry, and it profited them for the time, but...they are dead. Scarcity or prosperity, it is all one now. But with his eternal gifts it is not so. Lord, evermore give us this bread; to every generation of Christian people alike he offers the unlaborious dole that is to

Sacrament Most Holy

strengthen them for their spiritual journey, his flesh and his blood in the sacrament of Holy Eucharist. Shall we not learn to value it, we, to whom the value of earthly commodities has grown so small?

If thou knewest the gift of God! If we could only find some standard, but there is no standard, which would compare earthly things with heavenly; if we could only measure, but there are no terms in which to measure, what it is that we miss when we go to communion seldom, grudgingly, and indevoutly. No, you cannot estimate the value of such a gift by any human standard, and least of all by a standard we are accustomed to use in daily life, the standard of rarity. We confuse value with price; we think that because a thing is difficult to come by it is worth a great deal, that because the opportunities of enjoying a thing are rare, no such opportunity should be lost. God forgive us, we despise his graces because he has made them so cheap for us; the heavenly bread which is offered us without money and without price we put down, for that reason, as not worth having! That is not the law of the divine economy. All the graces bestowed on our blessed Lady and the saints, all the visions and the ecstasies and the power of working miracles, are not to be compared in value with what he gives us in holy communion; for that is himself. This gift, which is himself, is not for the few, but for everybody. *O res mirabilis, manducat Dominum pauper, servus et humilis*: we are all paupers in his sight, all slaves, all creatures of earth, and he will make no distinctions between us. He only asks that we should purge our consciences of mortal sin, and so come to him, asking him to bring just what he wants to give us, just what he knows that we need. "I am he who bade this be done; I will supply what is lacking to thee; come, and receive me."

XIV

The Mass and the Mass

Eastward then he faced, measured a thousand paces, and led me across a stream that reached my ankles. Another thousand, and when I crossed the stream it reached my knees; another thousand, and it was up to my waist; another thousand, and now it had become a torrent I might not cross any longer. Mark it well, son of man, said he. (EZECH. 47:3–6)

THE PROPHET EZECHIEL, during the exile in Babylon, had a vision in which he saw the temple precincts rebuilt; not on the old scale, but according to divine specifications; a plan which as a matter of history was never realized. Very painstakingly, an angel with a measuring rod in his hand conducts the prophet all round the sacred enclosure, till our heads swim as we read it in the effort to retain some picture of it in our minds. Then, suddenly, at the end of it all, he catches sight of a trickle of water, flowing out eastwards from the threshold of the temple itself. A trickle at first, but (as we have seen) it grows deeper; flows eastwards still, out into the desert, into the Dead Sea and beyond it, cleansing those waters by its passage. "Wherever it flows, there shall be teeming life again…and on either bank of the stream fruit-trees shall grow of every kind; never

---

This sermon was preached during the Holy Year.

Sacrament Most Holy

leaf lost, never fruit cast; month after month they shall yield a fresh crop, watered by that sanctuary stream; fruit for man's eating, and medicinal leaves" (Ezech. 47:12).

The Church, as we know, has borrowed that allegory for her use in Easter-tide; it shall be the type for her, of that new life which springs from our Lord's Resurrection; and all through Easter-tide, instead of the *Asperges* before Mass, we have the *Vidi aquam* of Ezechiel's vision (Ezech. 47). Shall we turn that allegory into a type of something not very different, the blessings which flow from the Holy Eucharist? You can see for yourselves that it would be possible, if we had time, to draw out the parallel in detail. But I thought, just for this evening, we would confine ourselves to one aspect of the picture; I mean the contrast between the tiny stream that flows out at the temple doors, and the great river into which it broadens out all at once. The Holy Mass is something so intimate, we are so snug within the four walls of a church, cut off from the noisy coming and going of humanity. And yet, if we allow ourselves to think about it for a moment, how the echoes of it, the ripples of it, fill the world!

So intimate, surrounded by all the furniture of piety which suggests nothing but holy thoughts; the hushed voice of the priest, his restrained gestures; the little mementoes I keep in my prayer-book, mortuary cards and a few favourite devotions; how nice to be alone for a little! And when I go to communion, how everything conspires to make it a private encounter with our blessed Lord—his body given for *me*, as if there were nobody else, preserving *my* soul, as if that were the only thing that mattered! Even we priests, who ought to know better, are tempted to cultivate this atmosphere

RONALD KNOX

of friendly isolation; we talk about "my Mass." *My* Mass—how "mine"? How could the Holy Mass belong to anybody? But there it is; for this one half-hour in the day we are guaranteed against interruption from other people, their troubles, their grievances, their sins; with the words *Introibo ad altare Dei* we have gone behind a curtain and fenced the world off from us; we are shut in with a limited sphere of familiar action, symbolical gestures are the cushion of our thoughts; the server is there, ready to hand us the next thing we want, our *Dominus vobiscum* sets up the expected echo of response. *Solus cum solo*, at last we are alone with God; we who ought always to be alone with him, yet somehow manage to forget him, because we are so busy in his service.

If a priest were wrecked, all by himself, on a desert island, and by some incalculable chance had all the requisites for Mass ready to hand, I suppose he would be justified in saying Mass, day after day, without even a server to share in the exercise. And still, day after day, he would find himself interceding not only for himself but *pro omnibus circumstantibus*, for all the people standing round; he would turn and bid them ask acceptance for this sacrifice, his sacrifice and theirs; he would ask God to remember, together with his own, the intentions of the bystanders; and all the while there would be no answer to his Mass except the lapping of the waves and the cry of sea-gulls. I wonder if he wouldn't be impressed, merely by this ironical contrast, with the fact which ought to impress us whenever we go to Mass, but all too seldom does; that the Mass is essentially a corporate affair, a family affair, in which the priest is meant to stand out against a background of faithful laity; in which the laity ought to have the sense of sharing God's mercies with all

Sacrament Most Holy

the people round them, even with the woman who has taken their favourite seat, even with the man who looks as if he had come to rob the poor-box? The Mass is not just me worshipping; I am part of a crowd, the crowd of *circumstantes*, who are making, by their concerted action, a joint offering to almighty God.

If only people heard Mass at their own parish churches, I think we might realize that more clearly than we do. In a small country congregation, where the people are all neighbours and mostly related to one another, you do sometimes get the sense of the Mass as it ought to be, a family affair. One of the antiphons for Corpus Christi Day tells us that the children of the Church ought to be like sturdy olive branches round the Lord's table, a reminiscence from that beautiful psalm which gives you such a glimpse of harmonious family life. The priest is the father of his congregation; not only in the sense that he adopts them at the font, not only in the sense that he corrects their faults in the confessional; he is the bread-winner, welcoming his children and dividing up their portions to them. A family meal is not meant to be like a *cafeteria*, where you sit reading your newspaper and glaring at the other people; it is a common feast of unity, everybody conscious of a common relationship to their father and to one another. And when we go to Mass, although we don't need to be looking round and seeing what other people are wearing or wondering why they are late, we ought to be generally conscious of our fellow worshippers as forming part of a unity, in which unity we and they as a family are approaching almighty God.

That is our first step, then, out into the stream of the prophet's vision. The Mass is not just that shallow trickle—you can hardly call it more—of your own pious thoughts, your own aspirations to be made one with Christ. It is already a mountain torrent, swirling round your knees and bidding you be careful not to lose your footing. But is that all? No, absent friends come into the picture too. The priest is not allowed to offer the sacrifice merely for himself and for the congregation. He tells God that he is offering it for the bystanders themselves and also for their intentions on behalf of other people, *pro se suisque omnibus*. The people who are too old or too ill to go to Mass, the people who are too busy to go to Mass, even the people who could perfectly well go to Mass but for some reason don't go to Mass, all form part of the shadow family that is gathered round the Lord's table. When you begin to remember *that*, to remember that you are charged with the weight of everybody else's special intentions as well as your own, you do begin to take the strain; you are like St Christopher crossing the stream, with the holy Child feeling more and more of a weight on his back. Or, to stick more closely to our original metaphor, you find that the stream is flowing waist-high, breast-high; you are a mere struggling unit in the tide of intercession. The Mass is no longer your Mass, as you fondly thought of it; the church is crowded to suffocation with all the people who might be there, you and they all struggling to get to heaven together, helping one another on. There's no end to it.

But there is worse yet to come. The priest doesn't simply recall before God the needs of the people who are there in church, and the needs of the people they are interested in; you suddenly find that this Mass, your Mass, is being offered for all faithful people, all over the world. And with that, the stream has grown so full that it carries you away altogether, quite out of your depth. The walls of the church seem to enlarge, the altar, instead of being a few feet

Sacrament Most Holy

away, becomes a mere speck in the distance; it isn't *a* church any longer, it's *the* Church, the holy Catholic Church, that bounds your horizon, and what is happening there is not *a* Mass, it's *the* Mass, the one sacrifice that is going on all over the world, of which this Mass, your Mass, is only the pin-point, focused at a particular moment of time, within a particular determination of space. Your family worship is not merely that of the parish; it's the worship of the whole Christian family, and you are there with the Hottentots and the Laplanders, children of the same family, met round the same table. More distant presences come to mind; our Lady and the saints and the faithful departed. But even without them, how vast a thing our family worship is seen to be!

And the Father of that common family? We name him in the Mass; our Father, Pius. Do not think that the Holy Year is merely a device for increasing the tourist traffic; do not think that the intentions of the Church in proclaiming it are sufficiently realized when millions of people are transported, by mere locomotion in space, to a particular built-up area called Rome. No, the journey which pilgrims take there is meant to be simply an attestation of loyalty; loyalty to the person of the Holy Father, and in his person to the whole idea of Catholic unity. Go to Rome this year merely to see the sights, and your visit is laudable enough, but you have missed the spirit of the occasion; it was love, not curiosity, that was meant to draw you. And if, for whatever reason, you have decided not to go to Rome this year, that does not mean the Holy Year has no meaning and no message for you. So many millions of Catholics in the world that cannot be present at the Confessio; not one of them but can take part in the Holy Year by letting his heart go out to the Father of Christendom. Every time you go to Mass, when the priest's voice dies away into silence after the *Sanctus*, that is your cue. Offer, in union with the priest, your own prayers for our Father Pius, father of the whole family, and his intentions. The Pope's intentions, how lightly those words fall on the ear, like a mere rigmarole, a mere formula! Have you ever thought what it would be like to be the Holy Father, to take, for a single day, for a single hour, the strain of his world-wide office? When you pray for the Pope's intentions at Mass, take your stand beside him in imagination, the man on whom we Christians, millions of us, have laid the burden of our common solicitudes. Plunge yourself, for a moment, in that full tide of prayer which is the prayer of the Church universal; then, if you will, scramble up the bank again, and return to the intimacy, the solitude of the Mass you are offering, just you and a few friends about you, nothing else to distract your thoughts from God. Your own prayer will ring truer, strike deeper, if just for a moment you have faced the glare, and felt the burden.

XV

The Pattern of His Death

So it is the Lord's death that you are heralding, whenever you eat this bread and drink this cup, until he comes. (1 Cor. 11:26)

THE THEOLOGY OF ST PAUL has not come down to us in the shape of carefully thought out catechetical instructions. It tumbles out of him at haphazard, by a series of providential accidents, when he is not meaning to talk about theology, but is devoting himself to the practical needs of the moment. It is to a providential accident that we owe his wonderful chapter on the Holy Eucharist, which is the basis of so much that we know, so much that we believe, about the sacrament of the altar. St Paul did not set out to extend the knowledge, or to confirm the faith, of the Corinthian church on that subject. No, it all comes out incidentally, when he is trying to correct certain abuses which had sprung up among those very half-baked converts of his in a rather easy-going seaport town. In those days the Christians used to meet for a common meal, which served as a preface to the celebration of the divine mysteries. And the meal was meant to be a share-out; everybody, rich or poor, brought what he could and divided it with his brethren. But at Corinth the richer and the more leisured folk used to come early, before the rest, and get through the good things they had brought, in agreeable solitude.

RONALD KNOX

It was turning into a boisterous convivial party, their preparation for Holy Mass, and St Paul, in recalling them to a sense of decency, points out among other things that their merriment is ill-suited to an occasion which must, in some sense, be an occasion of mourning. You cannot receive communion without associating yourself with a death. You are heralding the *death* of Jesus Christ, until he comes again.

Until he comes—when he used those words, what kind of perspective opened out, do you suppose, before St Paul's imaginative view? I think, if you had asked him, his guess would have been that it could not be very long now before his Master returned in glory. Everywhere, in that Mediterranean world he knew, the gospel had sprung up overnight, like the mustard-plant in the parable; everywhere the defences of the old gods were beginning to crumble, as they had crumbled at Corinth. There was as yet no persecution, except what was raised by Jewish incredulity; and could that incredulity last? At the moment, indeed, there was a veil over the hearts of his fellow countrymen, which mysteriously made them blind to the truth, while the Gentiles outstripped them in the race for salvation. But surely it could not be long before the Jewish people accepted the gospel; theirs were the promises, for them in the first instance Christ had died; and, day by day, whenever the Christian mysteries were celebrated, that death was heralded anew—surely it must avail them? Then, when Jew and Gentile alike had had their chance—in a few years, why not?—the skies would open, and the living Christ would come down, to judge the world which the dying Christ had ransomed.

Whatever be the truth about that, however little St Paul may

Sacrament Most Holy

have guessed that there was a long panorama of history still awaiting mankind, of this at least we can be certain, that the Spirit who spoke through St Paul bade him write those words for our comfort, so far removed in time, living in a world so altered. Till he comes—age after age must pass, and still the Church must suffer a hundred deaths as she heralded, with a kind of despairing confidence, the death of the Master who still did not return. At dead of night she would herald it, in the long subterranean passages that run mysteriously beneath the outskirts of Rome; slaves and patricians met together under the pretence that they were a burial club, among pagan tombs, pagan altars. In secret rooms of old country-houses she would herald it, in remote fastnesses of the hills, when our fathers were persecuted, and priests put to death, for love of the Mass and of the old ways. In foul prisons and concentration camps she would herald it, where some handful of deported Catholics had managed to collect the bare essentials for a valid sacrifice. And still he would not return.

What did St Paul mean, when he told us that in receiving holy communion we are heralding the Lord's death? When we kneel before the relics of some martyr, of Oliver Plunkett at Drogheda or John Southworth at Westminster Cathedral, we are, in a sense, heralding his death. We are reminding ourselves, and the same time we are acknowledging before the world, that this man's death was more worthwhile than any other kind of death; that the suffering which it cost him was the supreme proof of his loyalty, was a title to glory. In recognition of that, we venerate and salute with our lips those mortal remains of his from which death parted him, which he has left behind to us as a trophy of his victory. The saint

RONALD KNOX

himself is not here, or not here more than anywhere else; the bones we touch were once part of him, will be part of him once more at the General Resurrection; we do not doubt that (under God's providence) a grace and an influence still clings to them which may bring us help in our needs. The saint is alive, but in heaven; all we have got here is a dead body. No matter; it is the man's death we are heralding, and it is appropriate that we should do that by putting ourselves in contact with that dumb part of him which itself recalls the manner of his dying.

Is that what St Paul means? Does he imply that we receive, in holy communion, the dead body of Jesus Christ? It would be a very ill-instructed Catholic who would accept such a conclusion. On the contrary, what you and I receive in holy communion is precisely the risen body, the living body of Jesus Christ. If our hearts burn within us as we come away from the altar, it is because we, like the two disciples on the Emmaus road, have been offering hospitality to the risen Christ, though hidden under a form in which we could not recognize him. The risen body, which could defy the laws of nature, has passed into us, so that we may be energized by its supernatural power. The risen body, which went up to heaven in the sight of the apostles, has passed into us, so as to plant in us the seed of immortality. It is the risen body of Christ that reigns there over the altar; how should it be his dead body? There is no such thing; there never has been any such thing except during the brief interval between the first Good Friday afternoon and Easter morning. When we venerate the relics of a saint, we see him there, but in death. When we venerate Christ on the altar, he lives there, but lives unseen.

Sacrament Most Holy

How is it then that St Paul tells us we are heralding the death of Christ when we communicate? St Paul of all men, who of all men was most conscious of Christ's death as a transaction done and finished with, a door shut and slammed on the past? St Paul, who wrote, "Christ, now he is risen from the dead, cannot die any more" (Rom. 6:9); St Paul, who wrote "Even if we used to think of Christ in a human fashion, we do so no longer" (2 Cor. 5:16)—why does he tell us that we are heralding the death of Christ when we communicate, instead of saying the life of Christ, the Resurrection of Christ? We should find it hard to understand his attitude, if we had not the Christian tradition to fill up the gaps in his thought. Christian tradition teaches us that the Holy Eucharist does not merely consist in the consecration of the elements and their reception by the faithful; it is something more, it is a sacrifice. And because it is a sacrifice it involves, somehow, the death of a victim, and the application of that death to our needs. What is heralded in these mysteries is Christ dying, not Christ dead.

Christ dying—oh, to be sure, as a matter of history, Christ could only die once; it is given to men to die once for all, and he was Man. And you may say if you will that the sacrifice of the Mass is only the echo, only the ripple, set up day after day, century after century, by the sacrifice made once for all on the cross. An echo, a ripple, those are pleasing and perhaps helpful metaphors, but they are only metaphors; the sacrifice of the Mass is a mystery, and perhaps its relation to the sacrifice on the cross is the most mysterious thing about it. Only this is certain, that the victim who is there presented to the eternal Father for our sakes is the dying Christ; it is in that posture that he pleaded, and pleads, for our salvation, atoned, and atones, for the sins of the world. We herald that death in the Holy Mass, not as something which happened long ago, but as something which is mystically renewed whenever the words of consecration are uttered. From the moment of his death on Calvary until the time when he comes again in glory, the dying Christ is continually at work, is continually available. It is in this posture of death that he pleads for us, when the Mass is offered. And it is in this posture of death that he comes to you and me when he comes to us, the living Christ, in holy communion. "This is my body which is being given for you…this is my blood which is being shed for you"; so he spoke to his apostles when his death still lay in the future, so he speaks to us now that his death lies in the past.

What wonder if the Church, heralding his death from day to day, has caught something of this, his victim character? That life-cycle which he underwent in the natural body he took from our blessed Lady, he undergoes anew in his mystical body, which is the Church. St Paul knew that, from the moment when he fell dazzled on the Damascus road, and heard a voice saying to him, "Saul, Saul, why dost thou persecute me?" He rejoiced in his own sufferings, because they helped to "pay off the debt which the afflictions of Christ leave still to be paid, for the sake of his body, which is the Church" (Col. 1:24). How often, nowadays, men tell us in a half-pitying, half-contemptuous tone that we belong to a dying religion! Let us accept the omen, let us boast of the accusation; we are, we always have been, a dying religion. From the first, we went underground in the catacombs; again and again we have been forced to our knees, fought a losing battle all down the centuries; do they think it is any news to us that the world is our enemy; persecutes

Sacrament Most Holy

us as it persecuted our Master? Today as yesterday, she is content to herald his death until he comes.

And you and I, how do we come into the picture? Surely when we go to communion, we ought to reflect among other things, "This is his body which is being given for me; this is his blood which is being shed for me—after all this lapse of time, he still comes to me in the posture of a victim. And he wants to impress something of himself on me; I am to be the wax, he the signet-ring. Something, then, of the victim he wants to see in me; does not the *Imitation* say it is up to every Christian to lead a dying life?[1] Not for me, perhaps, to enter very deeply into the dispositions of my crucified Saviour, but…to be rather more humble, when I am thwarted; rather more resigned, when things go wrong with me; rather less anxious to make a chart of my own spiritual progress, more ready to let him do in me what he wants to do, without letting me know about it! If I could only die a little, to the world, to my wishes, to myself; be patient, and wait for his coming, content to herald his death by dying with him!"

---

1. *Imitation of Christ*, Book II, ch. 12, 14.

XVI

The Challenge

This is my body, on your behalf. (1 Cor. 11:24)

THE CHRISTIAN LITURGY seems to have grown up at haphazard, on no principle, every age leaving some mark on its development until it was crystallized four centuries ago. All the more strange, and (perhaps we may say) all the more obviously providential, that the phrases and the ceremonies of the Mass—antiquated, you would think, not designed by men of our world, or for the needs of our day—should so often exactly hit off our spiritual mood, say exactly the thing we wanted to say! There are moments, aren't there, in the Mass at which you catch your breath in surprise over what seems to be—what would be, in any human document—superb dramatic skill.

One of those moments is when the priest, having absolved the communicants, turns round with the sacred Host, and doesn't give it to them. They must be kept waiting, while he says three times the *Domine non sum dignus*. He treats them as if they were children, impatient for some treat which has been promised them, and needing to be taught patience by finding, just for a little, that the treat is held back. We thought we had prepared ourselves for holy communion so carefully—examining our consciences, perhaps going

Sacrament Most Holy

to confession, saying a lot of prayers and making a lot of acts, as the book told us to, and here we are at last at the altar rails, all ready; but no, it seems we were not ready. Lord, I am not worthy, Lord, I am not worthy, Lord, I am not worthy, even now. And perhaps during that tantalizing interval while the priest holds out to our view, but still will not give us, the bread of life, we do well to imagine that it is not the priest who is speaking in our name, it is our Lord himself speaking to us, asking us for a welcome, and at the same time warning us what that welcome involves.

Curiously, no one can tell us with certainty what words our Lord used when he, the first Christian priest, stood there in the cenacle offering his own flesh to his disciples. "This is my body on your behalf"—I am quoting from the earliest account we have of the scene, given us by St Paul in his first letter to the Corinthians; I am quoting it in the form in which it has been preserved by our oldest manuscripts. "My body on your behalf"—the phrase was a mysterious one, and it was natural that copyists should try to fill it out and make sense of it, some writing "my body which is being broken for you," and others, "my body which is to be given up for you." But it looks as if our Lord simply said, "My body on your behalf," not tying it down to the moment at which he spoke, nor to the foreseen moment of his betrayal. It was, indeed, when it was broken on the cross that the body of Christ became most evidently and most significantly ours. But all his life—that, I think, is what he wants us to see—all his life, from the moment when that body was formed in the womb of his virgin Mother, it existed on our behalf. *Propter nos homines*, for the sake of us men he came down from heaven, and took upon himself the outward fashion of a man; and this body of his was not merely to be the victim of our redemption; it was to be the means and the model of our sanctification from first to last.

This is my body (he says) on your behalf. God is all spirit; man is matter and spirit, but the bodily part of him is all matter. And therefore, when God becomes man, it would not be so extraordinary that he should take upon himself a human soul, which, after all, is spirit; but a body! This is the low-water-mark of our Lord's condescension; the abiding trophy, therefore, of his achievement. By taking a human body at all how utterly did he, who was pure spirit, dispossess himself! But that was not enough; it should be fashioned and grown as our human bodies are fashioned and grow; it should be a prisoner in the womb, it should have the inarticulate needs of childhood. All that experience it went through, this body of mine which you see in the hands of my priest; it was dressed in rough clothes, nourished with the simple necessities which are not denied to the poor. And you, who would receive it, you, who would be made one with it—are you ready to be made like me in my humiliation? Are you ready to be made one with me in poverty, enduring privations, content with the company of simple folk? Are you ready to be made one with me in my helplessness, accepting, with no murmur of pride, the good offices of your fellow men? Are you ready to be made one with me in the darkness of the womb, clinging to me by faith, when you can see nothing but night around you? That is what it means, if I come to you.

This is my body (he says) on your behalf. The body which he took upon himself when he became incarnate for our sakes was, as we have seen, the body of his humiliation; its movements, restricted

Sacrament Most Holy

by space and time, were a poor vehicle, in themselves, for the activities of the Eternal. And yet—so transfigured is everything by the touch of the Divine—this weak body became the accomplice of the wonders our Lord performed on earth. That hand, a hand like yours or mine, had only to touch the sick and they were cured; a glance from that eye could strike his persecutors to the ground; that voice had only to speak a word of invitation, and the dead man came out from four days' sojourn in the tomb. *Theandric* action, we call it, when all that is most human in the Incarnate is associated with the achievements that are most divine. And we, as we look up and see the priest holding out that body towards us, are comforted by the assurance that its powers are not exhausted; no ailment of our souls, no blindness, no feebleness, which cannot be healed by its contact. Yes, but that body, when it laboured for us on earth, was not sustained by any native strength beyond human strength, yours or mine; it was weary, as yours or mine might be, when he rested it by Jacob's well. Only the sanctified will which was in command of it could make it bear up under those long journeyings, against the constant strain of the multitudes thronging round it. "Virtue has gone out of me," he said; each miracle took its toll of that frail human organism. He never spared it; and we are so sparing with our bodies; give in so easily to their slightest murmur of complaint! Are you ready (he asks us) to be made one with me in my constant defiance of fatigue, to pray, to work, to face new situations, resolute and unflagging, as I did? That is what it means, if I come to you.

This is my body (he says) on your behalf. Most of all, when it was betrayed, when it was broken for our sakes; when it exchanged activity for passivity. How hard that is! And that is what the Passion meant, almighty God letting things happen to him. He let them hurry him away, bound and helpless, from Gethsemani to the council-chamber, from the council-chamber to the praetorium, from the praetorium to the cross. He let them nail him to the cross, those feet which tired on the roads of Galilee idle now, that hand which had so often reversed our human tragedies motionless. It was as if he wanted us to see that the greatest act of all his life was what he did when he seemed powerless to do anything. Tied hand and foot, he could still pardon, and absolve, and love. And now he rests motionless in the hands of his priest, carried this way and that at the discretion of human wills, but still pardoning, still absolving, still loving. We cannot fail to recognize, we cannot afford to ignore, this third challenge which our Lord's body throws down to us. Suffering is our common lot; it awaits all of us sooner or later, some of us in forms that may be acute and prolonged. And what makes it more than ever hard to bear is the feeling of helplessness; we have not willed this, it has been forced on us, and pride offers no consolation. To let ourselves suffer, only because it is his will; to let ourselves suffer, perhaps, as he did, from the neglect and the cruelty and the contempt of our fellow men—that is the chief, and perhaps the hardest thing he asks of us. But he does ask it of us. That is what it means, if I come to you.

I have been suggesting that when the priest, just before communion, says the threefold *Domine non sum dignus* in your name, you should imagine our Lord himself as holding back, keeping you waiting for a little, so as to test your dispositions. He often did that, didn't he, before consenting to perform a miracle; he told the Syrophoenician woman, "It is not right to take the children's bread and throw it to the dogs." He told St Martha, "Thy brother will rise again." Even to our Lady he said, "My time has not come yet." But, when I speak of testing our dispositions, do I mean that he looks into our hearts and expects to find his own likeness already there? Must we already be humble with a humility like his, already be unwearied in his service, already be perfectly resigned to all the sufferings which may befall us, or be told that we are not fit to receive him? If I meant that, if I meant that holy communion is a privilege reserved, at least commonly, for an élite of almost perfect souls, then I should be falling back into the error of the Jansenists, and I should be wronging the memory of that great Pope who has just been raised to the altars of the Church. For whatever else St Pius the Tenth is remembered, he will be remembered for having thrown open the gates of the sanctuary to hesitating and struggling souls; to the unworthy who know themselves to be unworthy.

No, the dispositions I am speaking of are not those which qualify us to receive holy communion; we go to holy communion in order that those dispositions may be formed in us. Only, we must *want* them to be formed in us. The trouble, you know, about you and me is not that we aren't saints, but that we don't want to be saints. Lord, I am not worthy, because I am not humble; but I do want to be humble. Lord, I am not worthy, because I am backward and slothful in your service; but I hate my backwardness, I hate my sloth. Lord, I am not worthy, because I am a bad sufferer; but how I wish it were otherwise! Let it be otherwise, Lord; speak the word only, and thy servant shall be healed.

XVII

A Better Country

We have an everlasting city, but not here. (HEB. 13:14)

WHAT A CHILLING EXPERIENCE it is to stand, as we stand today, on the morrow of a great occasion! Two days ago, only two days ago, the thing was happening; history was shaping itself under our view. And on a scale, I suppose, hitherto unparalleled; no human being has ever been watched by so many eyes simultaneously as Queen Elizabeth was on Tuesday morning. Oh, to be sure, our modern vulgarity had done its best to ruin the sacredness of it; there was a wealth of false sentiment, and of hysterical propaganda. But behind all that, behind all the masquerade and the publicity, you felt a perfectly genuine reaction of popular enthusiasm; each of us looked at his neighbour's face, and saw his own embarrassed loyalty reflected there. For one brief hour, a world torn by dissension stood agreed; all alike would do homage to a young woman, born to accept homage with a kind of natural grace. The streets which are so familiar to us, in which we jostle our way through a meaningless crowd of unrelated humanity, had turned overnight into a river-bed, through which a dazzling stream of pomp went

---

This sermon was preached in the week of her Majesty's Coronation.

Sacrament Most Holy

by; and we shouted and waved like school-children, all our anxieties, all our grievances, momentarily forgotten. Time stood still, and the care-lined features of this modern age were rejuvenated by the experience.

Only two days ago; and now it is all over, and we are fain to distract ourselves with the fireworks. The decorations hang limply, waiting to be taken down; we look at them half-ashamed, like a schoolboy confronted with the toys of childhood. All our pomp of yesterday is one with Nineveh and Tyre—the gaping crowds still eddy to and fro in the streets of London, but with a sense of anticlimax. After all, the Queen we crowned two days ago wields no powers she did not wield, commands no loyalty she did not command, before the ceremony took place. We are back where we were, just as anxious as before over yesterday's problems; can the world's peace be kept? How is our trade balance going to recover? What is to be the next step in Korea, in Egypt, in South Africa, all the world over? We have awoken from a dream of chivalry to the hard facts of real life. But it is not simply that the thing has come to an end, and we are sorry it could not last. We look back on our great moment, and somehow find it unsatisfying. What lies at the root of our disillusionment?

One ceremony our English Coronation lacks, for all its splendid history; a ceremony which takes place, as far as I know, only at the crowning of a Pope, I mean, when a bundle of tow is burned in his presence, to the accompaniment of those famous words—nobody knows where they come from, who invented them—*sic transit gloria mundi*, "So passes the glory of this world." Man was born for eternity, and every experience of his, when he comes to look at

RONALD KNOX

it afterwards, is found to be unsatisfying, not simply because it was impermanent, but because all the while it was imperfect. The crown which we set on the royal forehead is only, after all, a collection of mineral products, prized because there are not more of them. And the Queen herself, though she rightly claims the obedience and the homage of her subjects, is only a human creature like ourselves; she eats and drinks and catches cold and feels bored like the rest of us. When we crown her, we crown her as the symbol of the divine authority, of which she is the representative on earth; and we would crown her, if we could, not with mineral deposits, but with the imperishable glories of heaven. If we are haunted by a sense of unreality about Tuesday's proceedings, it is not that we regret what we have done. It is only that all our earthly experiences are, of their very nature, unsatisfying, and this, the most splendid experience of our lives, is unsatisfying like the rest—so dazzling to the eye, so challenging to the imagination, and yet, like all the things of time, it has eluded us, and is gone!

Man is born for eternity, and the horizons of a fallen world are too little for him. Always he tries, and fails, to express himself fully in his earthly surroundings, like some noble beast in captivity, that grows accustomed to its prison bars, yet never ceases to chafe at them. The lover feels, in his first flush of happiness, as if his love was something immortal, indestructible, only to see his romance fade into commonplace. The artist hails the inspiration that has come to him as something almost divine; once it has been committed to paper or to canvas, it no longer contents him. Always we are striving after the unattainable, and achieving the imperfect. Man—fallen man—is a misfit, an exile from his true country. It is that

Sacrament Most Holy

note of exile which has imposed itself, from the first ages, on the language of the Christian Church. We cry to our heavenly Queen as "poor *banished* children of Eve." "After this our *exile,*" we say, "show unto us the blessed fruit of thy womb." It was St Peter himself who gave us the cue for it, "Beloved, I call you to be like strangers and exiles." It was a familiar metaphor, God knows, to his fellow countrymen. The whole history of the Jewish race has been a history of exile; exile in Egypt, exile in the wilderness, exile in Babylon; and their whole literature is permeated with a sense of homesickness to which we, Christian people, have given a new meaning. "What, should we sing the Lord's song in a strange land?"—to the Jew, all the world was exile, away from Jerusalem; for us, there is no home except the new Jerusalem, and we shall not find it in this world. We have an everlasting city, but not here.

Does that mean that we are bad patriots, bad citizens of the British Commonwealth? God forbid that it should; God forbid that we should rake up memories of the past. For us, the institution of kingship is all the more real and all the more valuable because it is derived from, and symbolizes, the supreme power of almighty God; and in the same way the sentiment of patriotism is all the more real and all the more valuable because it is derived from, and symbolizes, that yearning love with which we look towards our heavenly country. Only, when we have witnessed all the pageantry of this last week, witnessed the homage that is paid by a multitude of nations, even in these dark days, to the historic continuity of the British crown, we must be pardoned if our afterthoughts bring with them something of melancholy. How should we not be reminded of that Jerusalem which is our true home, eternal in the heavens, whose gates stand ever open, while the nations flock into it with their honour and their praise? Citizens by right, we are not yet citizens in fact; we are only exiles, only displaced persons, in this world of sense and time. We are only strangers, with our faces set towards home.

If we are on a journey, we must have provisions. And the language of the liturgy leaves us in no doubt what those provisions are. *Esca viatorum*, the food of travellers, *per tuas semitas duc nos quo tendimus*, bring us, by thy own path, to our journey's end; *ecce panis angelorum factus cibus viatorum*, behold the bread of angels, sent to pilgrims in their banishment! *Qui vitam sine termino nobis donet in patria*, so may we pass eternity, poor exiles, on our native shore! The Holy Eucharist is our *viaticum*, our allowance of food at every stage in our travels; it is only by a gracious technicality that we reserve the name for that iron ration which will strengthen us for the last stage of all. Day by day and week by week, this is our appropriate nourishment. Not that the divine resourcefulness could not find other means of sustaining us. The prophet Elias went a journey of forty days through the wilderness in the strength given him by a single meal; and wherever there are faithful souls deprived, through no fault of their own, of sacramental opportunities, we do not doubt that God will provide them with all the graces they need. But normally it is the Holy Eucharist that will bring us to our journey's end, the day's food for the day's march, the heavenly manna we need, God knows we need it, on this parched earth.

The day's food for the day's march—shall we take comfort sometimes, from that thought, when we are disheartened over the miserably small effect which this heavenly nourishment seems to

Sacrament Most Holy

have on our lives? We are thinking of the Blessed Sacrament, you see, under another metaphor when we feel thus discouraged. We are thinking of it as the medicine which is meant to cure the disease of our souls; and more than that, to strengthen them, give them fuller, more robust health. And instead, our petty faults seem to go on unchecked, the meanness, the selfishness, the touchiness of our natures—how is it that they do not yield to treatment? Instead, our spiritual health seems to languish; we have no appetite for heavenly things, no energy for carrying out God's will even when we see it clearly enough—how is it that we still lack vigour, refreshed morning after morning with the bread of the strong? It is natural, it is right that we should sometimes ask ourselves these questions, but I think it is a mistake to be always feeling one's own pulse, always watching one's own symptoms. Let us be content, instead, to think of the Blessed Sacrament not as the medicine but as the food of our souls; acting on us, as material food does, without our knowing it, yet all the time sufficing for the day's needs, carrying us along on our journey, though we seem to make such a weary business of it, dragging foot after foot. The invalid who refuses food because it has so little relish for him becomes a worse invalid yet.

The food of pilgrims—shall we make use of those words to read ourselves, now and again, a different lesson? True enough, it is possible to fall into scruple by watching our own spiritual development too eagerly. But it is also possible to fall into carelessness by not watching our own spiritual development at all. Marching food is meant for the march, and you must have stretched your muscles if you are to enjoy it; how dull picnic fare tastes, if you are weather-bound, and compelled to eat in your arm-chair! "Your

RONALD KNOX

loins must be girt," our Lord says; we must be *bona-fide* pilgrims if we are to find our proper food in the Holy Eucharist. And it is so easy to forget, amid the distractions of the wayside, the country of our dreams. Hard enough, even in days gone by, to draw the mind away from the things of earth, and let them rest on the unseen things that are eternal. Always the gossip of your neighbours filled the ear; always the busy pageant of life displayed itself to the eye. And what of our age, when you may turn a switch, and listen endlessly to the jarring voices of a discordant world? Our age, when the eye can rest on a thousand images, good, bad, and indifferent, which are no better than shadows, yet the shadows of things seen? Of that everlasting city no sound, no sight can reach us. There, over the altar, our King is enthroned, but hidden under symbols, and in silence. And yet so close to us; closer than hands or feet.

XVIII

Jesus My Friend

Iron sharpens iron, and friend shapes friend. (Prov. 27:17)

IF YOU COME TO THINK OF IT, a priest who celebrates his jubilee has stood at the altar about nine thousand times. Supposing him just fifty years old, he was a boy of eight when Pius X gave us daily communion as a target for the ordinary faithful layman to aspire to. So he has probably made some fifteen thousand communions in his life; and there are many of the faithful laity who don't lag far behind. What a terrifying thought it is that the good Shepherd should have fed us so often with his own hand, and here are we still straying; that the good Physician should so often have asked, "Well, how are we this morning?" and we are still so weak!

Less discouragingly, let us think this evening of our eucharistic Lord as a Friend, a personal Friend. That title, after all, he claimed at the Last Supper, "I have called you my friends"; using, probably, a Hebrew word which throws into relief the reciprocity of human friendship, and thereby raising his apostles to a kind of equality with himself. A shepherd has so many sheep to look after, the doctor has so many calls to make; your friend, when he comes to see you, is at liberty, is at your disposal; he has "just dropped in." And our Lord wants each of us to think of him in that way; nor do we deceive ourselves if we think of him in that way. Infinite power, infinite goodness, makes itself infinitely available. Go to communion in some little country church, where you find yourself alone at the altar rails, or go to midnight Mass at Westminster Cathedral, and get sucked into the interminable queue which is slowly moving eastwards—it makes no difference. In either case the sacred Host which you are destined to receive contains the whole of Christ, all meant for you. "Is my friend there?" he is saying; waiting for you, like the person who comes to meet you at a crowded terminus, looking out for that particular trick of walking, that particular way of holding yourself, which will single you out at a distance.

Our friends—how they change, don't they? Those chance meetings on the Underground, when you sit chatting to someone who was your bosom friend years ago, and find yourself with very little to say except, "Wonder what's become of old So-and-so," and hoping that there will be enough old So-and-so's to last out till Charing Cross! And even with the friendships we make later in life, founded not on accidental association, but on a real community of tastes and interests, how seldom they last a lifetime, or anything like a lifetime! Destiny shuffles our partners for us; one friend or the other gets a different job, goes to live somewhere else; it may only mean changing from one suburb to another, but how easily we make an excuse of distance! More and more as we grow older, we find that the people we see most of are recent acquaintances, not (perhaps) very congenial to us, but chance has thrown them in our way. And meanwhile the people we used to know so well, for whom we once entertained such warm feelings, are now remembered by a card at Christmas, if we can succeed in finding the address. How

Sacrament Most Holy

good we are at making friends, when we are young; how bad at keeping them! How eagerly, as we grow older, we treasure up the friendships that are left to us, like beasts that creep together for warmth!

There is no difficulty of that kind with the Friend who makes himself known to us in the Blessed Sacrament; he is always at hand, always available. Do not complain that his friendship always feels unreal to you, feels impersonal to you, because he is hidden under sacramental veils. After all, what a sense of intimacy we derive simply from a friend's handwriting in a letter! It is only by a trick of memory that we associate it with his or her personality, and yet how near it brings us, this veil of handwriting! Even when you are sitting talking to a friend, you are not really talking *to* him; your mouth is talking to his ear, his mouth to yours; the play of expression on his features is nothing more than a twitching of muscles. Face and voice are only veils that hide the real person from you, and yet how easily you see behind those veils! And if we had faith, the sacramental veils under which our Lord comes to us would be lifting and parting all the while; we should get a much greater sense of nearness to him, under the token of eating bread, than we get when we are talking to a friend under token of watching the muscles of his face. Go about the world as you will, change your home as often as you will, in the nearest Catholic church your Friend is always there, and day by day he is at home to you.

It is not only distance that estranges us from our earthly friends. After all, how little we really *know* of one another! You meet a person for the first time, and you are charmed by some trick of manner, or you find some common topic of conversation which interests you, and you go home saying to yourself that it is really a great piece of luck to have met somebody who is so absolutely cut out for you. And yet it may take only a few weeks of further intercourse for each to discover a want of sympathy for the other's point of view, some tiresome mannerism that gets on one's nerves, and the friendship fades away into a bare acquaintance. We are changing, too, all the time, ever so little; habits grow upon us, new interests grip us; how easy it is even after years of friendship to find that the other person is not quite what you thought he was—or is it that you are not quite what you thought you were? Anyhow, an illusion has faded. But the Friend who comes to you in the Holy Eucharist is the same yesterday, today and for ever; and as better knowledge brings more intimacy, you can find nothing there but what will make his qualities more lovable. Or again, you may fall upon evil times, when poverty, or some suspicion cast on your character, lowers your standing in the world. Friends may desert you then; or, more likely, you will wrongly suspect them of deserting you, or you will shun their company because you think they are trying to patronize you. There is no need for such fears, there is no need for such pride, about our friendship with Jesus Christ. "Zacchaeus, come down, for today I must abide at thy house"; it is all arranged, the despised publican is to be our Lord's host. And he will invite himself in as our guest too, even when we despise ourselves, even when the world despises us. What a Friend to have, changeless himself, and never minding how much we change!

Always the same warmth of welcome from him, whatever coldness there has been on our part. Each day he makes good our wastage of yesterday, like a patient grown-up helping a child with

Sacrament Most Holy

its toys. Each day he offers us the whole of himself, infinite possibilities of sanctification, knowing that we shall make so little of them! And this strange condescension of his has been repeated so often that it has ceased to surprise us; hardly ever, apart from rare moments of recollection, engages our gratitude. Most of us have had the same experience with some unselfish friend—God be thanked for all such—who always gave much and asked little. The help, the sympathy, the little attentions we get from such a friend become a normal part of our daily lives, like the sun rising in the morning; we take them for granted. Then, perhaps, the friend is removed from us by death, and we remember with a sudden shock, "I shall never get those flowers from the country again!" or something of that sort. The friendship of our Lord in the Holy Eucharist is all the more easily forgotten, because the benefits which he bestows upon us are in the order of grace; we are not aware of them, we cannot count and check them. Sometimes, to be sure, there is an overflow of them into our feelings, but as a rule that is only something transient, and quite certainly it is something to which we ought not to attach a great deal of importance; one day we are all gratitude after communion, all floods of tears, and the next we are all dry and hard—what does it matter? All those feelings of ours are a mere echo, a mere by-product of divine grace; they are no more to be confused with grace itself than the humming of the wheels are to be confused with the work the machine is doing. The growth of grace in us through holy communion is something as secret, as silent, as the restoration of tissues which natural food brings to our bodies. Only over a long space of time, as a rule, can the effects of it be observed; and even then, probably, not by ourselves.

RONALD KNOX

"Yes, but is there really growth?" you ask. "If I look back over these last twenty years or so, I don't see that I'm much different, and what difference there is can't, I'm afraid, in some directions be regarded as an improvement. How am I to trace, how am I to assess, the progress I have made? You tell me not to trust my feelings; what other index can I find of my spiritual condition? Ought I to find that as the years go on my temptations grow fewer, grow weaker? Or that the temptations are the same, but I yield to them less? Or should I look round and see if I can catch myself doing unselfish actions which I probably shouldn't have done twenty years ago? It would strengthen my faith in the Holy Eucharist, if I could only watch the Holy Eucharist making a difference, from year to year, in my own life."

For goodness' sake don't talk like that. I'm sure we aren't meant to think of the grace of holy communion as something which can be gauged and weighed up in a balance and written down in the form of a debit and credit account. Do let us get it into our heads that holy communion is an intimacy with Jesus Christ, and that if we do our best to throw our hearts open to his Sacred Heart, there is bound to be an influence passing from him into us. It is the law of friendship.

Iron sharpens iron, says the wise man, and friend shapes friend. Literally the words run, "Iron sharpens iron, and friend sharpens the face of friend," but that is simply the Hebrew way of putting things. What it means, evidently, is that your friendship with So-and-so inevitably knocks you into a particular shape, just as one piece of iron knocks another into a particular shape if you hit them against one another. Inevitably, not as the result of any deliberate attempt on the part of either to influence the other, but simply as the result of daily contact. And of course, speaking of human friendships, I think the wise man had this in mind, that either affects the other equally; it's not like sharpening a pencil, which leaves the knife just as it was. But when we are speaking about the friendship of Jesus Christ, of course it is different. Nothing about us can influence him, there is nothing in him that needs to be influenced. If you come to think of it, I suppose he was the only person who ever came across our blessed Lady without being the better for it.... No, the influence is all on one side.

But on our side, shall we doubt the influence is there? How well we know it in ordinary life, the unconsciously received influence of friend on friend! The schoolgirl who adopts the handwriting of her favourite schoolmistress, the young man who picks up all the catch-words and tricks of speech that are used in his fiancée's family, and so on. And as we know, it cuts much deeper than that; nothing can inspire us, nothing can drag us down, like our friendships; and we aren't conscious of it happening. Do we doubt that an influence equally unconscious, and far stronger, attaches to the daily intimacy of Jesus Christ?

Jesus Christ, the same yesterday, today and for ever; that intimacy binds up our days in a gracious unity. We have changed so much, you and I; made so many false starts, picked up so many friends and drifted away from them; am I, are you, the same person as twenty years ago? Yes, it is the same now as then; you and I, now as then, are the unworthy friends of Jesus Christ.

XIX

First and Last Communions

What Jesus Christ was yesterday, and is today, he remains for ever.
(HEB. 13:8)

IN THE DOCTRINE about the presence of our Lord in the Holy Eucharist, we admit a single exception to a law of science. We admit there is something we come across in our experience which can communicate energy without losing energy in itself. Jesus Christ, the same yesterday, today, and for ever. When he moved on our earth, we know that a power went forth from him which influenced even the material conditions of things around him. When the woman who had an issue of blood came behind and touched his garment, he knew within himself (so the gospel puts it) that virtue had gone out of him. But we cannot suppose that this meant any diminution of the spiritual energies which informed his incarnate nature; the source of those energies was divine. And, since he has ascended into heaven, he has not withdrawn his incarnate presence from the natural order; he has only altered the manner of it. His body born of Mary, his blood shed on Calvary, remain present substantially on our altars under the forms of bread and wine; and thus from the heart of his material creation he continues to radiate that life-giving influence which was his in the days of his humiliation.

Sacrament Most Holy

Here then, once more, you have an energy which continually diffuses itself and never grows less. As the bush which Moses saw in the wilderness burned continually but was never consumed, so our Lord's body and blood, present to us in their substance, not in those accidents which are subject to physical laws of growth and decay, are inexhaustible in their perpetual operation.

Yesterday, today, and for ever—cast your mind back to the first Mass on the first Maundy Thursday. What the apostles received, what Peter, what Judas received, was not something other than you and I receive, centuries afterwards. True, every circumstance of history conspired to make that occasion memorable and unique. They were being housselled, as no man was ever housselled since, by the very hands of Incarnate God. It was a viaticum, his viaticum, not theirs; deriving its efficacy from a meritorious cause, his Passion, which was not yet in existence. It was the transition, perhaps as yet only dimly appreciated, from the bloody sacrifices of the old law to the one bloodless sacrifice of the new. But it was the same sacrament which you and I receive; with the same virtue, the same effects. It availed no more to sanctify Peter or to condemn Judas, than it avails to sanctify, or to condemn, you and me.

Yesterday, today, and for ever—cast your mind forward to the last Mass that will ever be said on earth. We find it even more difficult thus to transport ourselves into the future; there will be so many novelties, we feel, that we can form no idea of at present. It goes without saying that the Christian liturgy, already so venerable, is less likely than anything else to be modified by the hand of time. Yes, it will be the same in all essentials; but how are we to think of the priest, for example? A Chinaman, perhaps, or a New Zealand native. The language in which the vernacular prayers are said will be a language, perhaps, which the human race has not yet invented. The architecture of the church may be of a kind we can imagine as little as the holy apostles, say, could have imagined Westminster Abbey. The feast celebrated on that occasion may be the feast of some saint who will not be born for many years yet. Yes, it is only a dim picture to our minds—and now, think what it will mean. That Mass will be the world's viaticum; this perishable creation, or our experience of it at least, will have no tomorrow. Nay, if we may dare to put it so, that Mass will be the viaticum of the Holy Mass itself; it will never be needed again, for we shall have advanced from faith to sight, from shadows and images into the truth. *Ite, Missa est*, the priest will say, and there will never be Mass again. And yet, in the consecration of that last Mass the body and blood of our Lord Jesus Christ will be no more and no less present, no more and no less powerful in its effects, than in the Mass you are hearing just now, or in that first Mass of the first Maundy Thursday. That divine energy will remain inexhaustible, when all the wheels of creation threaten to run down.

We have taken a glance at the first page and at the last page of eucharistic history. We stand—where? Somewhere in between, with little right to judge how far we are removed from the later point. Only, there are certain periods in history, and this is one of them, when we are more than ordinarily conscious of great changes happening and threatening in human affairs. It may be that a new and better world order is coming to the birth. But we are more immediately conscious of something else; of failing energies (so it would appear) in those institutions which we thought

Sacrament Most Holy

were unalterable and undying. Is the principle of democracy to disappear? Will the British Empire survive? Will Europe continue to hold her own against those Eastern civilizations which hitherto she has defied? Some even doubt whether there are not signs of failing energy about the human genius itself; whether the race of great men is not dying out, and leaving the stage of history to pinchbeck figures that successfully attract the limelight.... No loss of power, perhaps, but a redistribution of it and a deconcentration of it, as if the second law of thermodynamics were at work on our human destinies too. In a world of shifting values, there is one fixed point on which our hearts can rest, one fixed star by which our intellects can be guided; it is the personal presence of our Lord on earth, yesterday, today, and as long as earth endures.

Do these long horizons frighten and baffle our imaginations? Then let us remember that each of our individual lives has its own eucharistic history too; can look back to its first communion, look forward to its last.

Your first communion—I am assuming that you were a Catholic from birth—was given you when you were something quite different; I had almost said somebody quite different, from what you are today. That small boy in an Eton collar, that small girl in white, is already so much a thing of yesterday that you almost wonder whether your life is indeed linked, by conscious continuity, with its own past; you scarcely feel concerned to defend your childhood's behaviour, to recall your childhood's thoughts. But it *was* you, at a different stage in the making; the guilt of those tiny sins, the merit of those tiny sacrifices, still live on your record. When you knelt, for the first time, at the communion rail, how different it all was from your communions now! The act, staled since by repetition, was for that child something entirely new and portentously solemn. The eye of faith was clearer, for all experience was fresh to you, and most information came by hearsay, so that you had hardly learned to puzzle over the mysteries of faith. And, with your character still half-formed, you had no legacy of sinful habits to make you unsure of yourself, doubtful of your loyalty to him who came to dwell in you.

You were different, yes; but the gift received that day was no other than the gift you receive now; no more and no less powerful to breed and to nourish the seed of sanctity in you. You received Jesus Christ, the same yesterday, and today, and for ever.

Your last communion—I am assuming that, by God's grace, you will end your life faithful to his service, and that you will leave it fortified by his sacraments. In some ways, your last communion will be like your first. I mean, that the choice of time will not be yours; that other people will be making all the arrangements for you, and that your part will be one of consent rather than one of active co-operation. Your attention, too, will be apt to wander; not this time, from the exuberance of life, but from the weakening of the mortal powers which the approach of death brings with it. In other ways, there will be a great difference between that child that was you and the old man, the middle-aged man, the young man, perhaps, that you will be. That clear faith of the child will not be yours; you will wish that it was, that it might lighten for you the transition from time into eternity. That clear conscience of childhood will not be yours; you will have to look back on many sins indifferently matched by contrition, on many opportunities wasted, many days mis-spent. You will feel, perhaps, for the first time, under that shadow, what holy communion really means, what all your communions ought to have meant and did not mean to you, since that hush of childish anticipation in which our Lord first came to you. But he, remember, will be the same; he will offer to you, at a moment when the richest gift in the world is no longer worth having, a gift surpassing all the riches of the world, himself. He who was yours yesterday, who is yours today, will offer himself then to be yours for ever.

Our natural powers, let us make no mistake about it, are subject to the same law I was alluding to just now; as life goes on, there is a dissipation of energy, a deconcentration of effort. Youth will fling itself into any ambition, however trumpery, as if with a lifetime's ardour; we burn for a cause, or live for an ambition, as if nothing else mattered. As we grow older, our minds broaden and our activities widen; we are no longer so one-sided in our enthusiasms. That is a gain, yes; but at the same time there is a loss of power; we no longer grasp our certitudes so clearly, bring such freshness to the pursuit of our ideals. But the supernatural habit of charity which the Blessed Sacrament implants and breeds in us escapes this law of impermanence; it has the unaging quality of that divine source it springs from. What greater blessing can I wish you, then, for this feast of yours, than that you should learn to make each communion with your first and your last communion before your minds; your first, that you may labour to recover those lost fervours; your last, that you may study to be found now as you would fain be found then, detached from earth and winged for your flight into eternity? The love which our divine Guest shows for us in this sacrament never alters, never wearies; shall we let it be said of us, as the years go on, that his love is the same, and ours has changed? May he rather grant us grace to receive him always as children in our simplicity, as dying men in the utter abandonment of ourselves to him.

XX

Pity for the Multitude

I am moved with pity for the multitude; it is three days now since they have been in attendance on me, and they have nothing to eat.
(MATT. 15:32)

THE MIRACLE OF THE FIVE THOUSAND is so familiar to us, that the miracle of the four thousand, which was performed soon afterwards, makes no clear impression on the mind. "We have heard all that before," we say to ourselves; "it is just the same story, only the statistics were different." But we are wrong; the whole situation is different. On that earlier occasion, the people who accompanied our Lord to the further side of the lake had only had a day's outing; nor had they gone far afield—it would still have been possible for them to buy food in the neighbouring villages. This time, the need is more urgent; crowds of people have followed him right out into the desert, and the scanty provisions they brought with them are already exhausted. The disciples, this time, do not pretend to have any solution of the difficulty. And our Lord looks round him, and is moved with pity for the multitude.

I am *moved* with pity—the translators, most of them, have missed a point here. "I am sorry for the crowd," or some such phrase as that, does not do justice to the original. For the verb used, a comparatively rare one, implies a sort of physical discomfort in the speaker; he experiences that sick longing which is sometimes evoked in us by the spectacle of human tragedy. We take no credit to ourselves for our sensibility; we want to do something about it merely by way of relieving our own feelings. And our Lord bears testimony, I think, to the completeness of his own humanity when he makes use of such a phrase; he professes himself, as it were, "got down" by the sight of all these people, invalids, many of them, faint for want of food. His divine beneficence is called into play by a natural feeling of revulsion which links him to our common humanity.

I am moved with pity *for the multitude*; his compassion, because it was human, was spontaneous; because it was divine, was on the grand scale. We find our hearts go out in compassion towards this or that victim of poverty or distress; when a whole crowd of people is affected, our sympathy—I mean our instinctive sympathy—grows fainter, just where it should have been redoubled; if a whole sub-continent is ravaged by pestilence or famine, we put our hands in our pockets, but we are too unimaginative to feel the tragedy. With our Lord, it is not so; he has been dealing with them one by one, these three days past, the blind, the dumb, the lame, the palsied, the possessed; and now, contemplating them *en masse*, he is as conscious as ever of their common need; he has pity on the multitude. His own bodily constitution was no different from ours, and for three days he has been hard at work, virtue going out of him with each miraculous operation; he must have been hungry. But he does not think of himself; he has pity on the multitude.

It is three days now since they have been in attendance on me—oh, it was their own fault. They should have waited till he came

Sacrament Most Holy

back from his travels, met him in Galilee, where he could have dealt with them at leisure. But no, the mere rumour of his coming has sent them flocking out into the desert, regardless of the embarrassments that will result. They have been inconsiderate, as men are commonly inconsiderate when their need is great. And how hard it is to be patient with inconsiderateness of this sort; how readily we excuse ourselves with the reflection, "Really they have no right to expect so much of me." But our Lord does not talk like that; he feels, in a sense, responsible for the predicament in which these people find themselves; it is through their attendance upon his movements that they find themselves so hungry now. Granted that they were swayed by self-interest, some of them in quest of health, others mere sight-seers, full of curiosity, it was nevertheless a kind of rudimentary faith that brought them so far from their homes; it is out of such material that his Church, later on, will be recruited. He is moved with pity—it makes him feel uncomfortable, that followers of his should be faint with exhaustion, just because they were his followers.

Corpus Christi Day reminds us that our Lord has ascended into heaven in his sacred humanity; it is superior, now, to all the accidents of mortality, but the gracious character of it remains complete. He is still in touch with us, his followers, through the power of his eucharistic life; and still, as in that desert place beyond the Lake of Galilee, he has pity on the multitude, all those thronging millions who crowd, so unworthily, about his table. Oh, to be sure, we have not forgotten that the divine nature is full of mercy; we cannot doubt that somehow, in God, all those perfections exist which we recognize as perfections in man. But God's ways are so difficult for us to understand; "I will show pity," he says, "on those whom I pity, I will show mercy where I am merciful"; only an insight into his long-term plans would enable us to comprehend the unequal distribution—so it seems to us—of his favours. We are more at home—put it in that way—in the contemplation of our Lord's Sacred Heart, still human, and still feeling for us in human fashion. We still crowd about him, like those Galileans, without shame or embarrassment, almost inconsiderately, crying out, "Don't forget *me*, Lord! My needs are so pressing; don't forget me!"

And still, in his eucharistic life, he pities us, makes allowances for us. Lest we should be in any doubt of that, he has given us proof of it in our lifetime, by the increased considerateness of holy Church for our human weaknesses. Those of us whose Catholic memories go back over forty five years can remember what it used to be like going to communion, perhaps, eight times in the year, and even so, how full of anxiety and of scruple! Were we certain that we had really repented of our sins? That this or that fault in us was a venial, not a mortal sin? That we had really given proper time to our preparation, that the distractions which thronged about us on our way to the altar were really involuntary? And then a saintly Pope, the tenth Pius, was filled with the spirit of his Master, and said, like his Master, "I am moved with pity for the multitude." For the multitude—for us work-a-day Christians, so painfully numerous, who fall short, all the time, of the Christian ideal. We were hungry for spiritual nourishment in a desert world, a world that had largely forgotten God, fallen in love with the pitiable illusion of human progress, and St Pius taught us that frequent and daily communion was not to be thought of as a rare privilege of the cloister,

Sacrament Most Holy

as the prize, jealously granted, for a life of uninterrupted devotion in God's service. It was to be our talisman against every-day temptations, our salve for every-day shortcomings. How natural it seems now; what a stir it created then!

Time has moved on since; and from the first it was clear that this ideal of frequent and daily communion offered its advantages only to the few. Schoolchildren could readily avail themselves of it, and old people who had retired, and that rapidly diminishing part of the population which lived in comparative leisure, cushioned by domestic help. But what of all the people who scrambled off, morning by morning, at the last moment, to work; what of nurses in hospitals, soldiers in barracks, and all those others who could not command their own time? To these, the eucharistic fast was still a difficulty not easily surmounted; for these even on feast days, and for some of them even on Sundays, there was neither time nor opportunity to approach the altar, without heroic sacrifice. And now, only the other day, the Holy Father has spoken again in Christ's name, "I am moved with pity for the multitude." The multitude—it was never the Church's wish that only a select few should meet at the common table; it was meant for all alike. And if the conditions under which we live and work interfere with the gathering of ourselves together, then the discipline of an earlier age must be relaxed; not for her to set limits to the compassion of Jesus Christ.

That compassion, mediated through his Church, meets us halfway; and shall we do nothing to welcome it? In mere gratitude, we are bound to avail ourselves of these new opportunities. Perhaps you have been content, for years past, to fulfil your paschal duties, and do no more or very little more about it; awkward working hours, distance from a church, uncertain health made it so difficult for you. The reason is gone now, and will you persist in the ungracious habit? Was the reason, after all, only an excuse?

Another thing. When going to communion meant getting up before breakfast, it seemed to create the right atmosphere. Assoiled by sleep from the distractions of yesterday, surrounded by the peaceful influences of early morning, we went out to receive the Christ who was born of a Virgin and at midnight rose at early dawn from a virgin tomb. Our cares, our passions, were in a manner sealed off; we were at leisure for holy thoughts. Let it not be supposed that the Church, when she allows us to approach the altar later in the day after a brief discipline of fasting, cares nothing about this recollectedness of which we are speaking, which used to come to us so naturally. Always we must avoid scruple; but we should be more careful than we were in old days to make a good preparation for holy communion, isolating our minds as far as possible from the day's solicitudes, and asking the Holy Spirit to make a home in us worthy of Christ's coming. It may be we shall not make a great success of it, but the effort must be there.

On all the multitudes who come to receive him, on all the multitudes who neglect him, may Christ have pity.

XXI

One Body

For we, being many, are one bread, one body, all that partake of Christ.
(1 Cor. 10:17)

THIS CONGREGATION, bound as it is by the title of its church to be a special focus of the eucharistic cult, is privileged to observe the devotion of the Forty Hours at the very time when the Church in general is celebrating the Corpus Christi feast. It is well to ask ourselves, therefore, what we mean by this devotion, and for what special purpose it was ordained. There is no time, and there is no need, in which the exposition of our Lord's body over the altar would not be efficacious in exciting the affections of Christian people. But when we celebrate the Forty Hours, we do it for a special purpose, and that purpose becomes evident the moment we consider the ceremonies which constitute it. Nobody who thinks about his prayers at all can have failed to ask himself: Why is it that the Mass on the second day of the Forty Hours is a Mass for Peace? And the answer is supplied by the very documents which first regularized and standardized this devotion. It was instituted in order to secure

---

This sermon was preached at Corpus Christi Church,
Maiden Lane, on the Feast of Corpus Christi, 1932.

concord among Christian princes, and safety from that Turkish menace which still, even in the sixteenth century, disturbed the tranquillity of Christendom.

You will not accuse me, then, of speaking beside the mark if I preach to you about the Blessed Sacrament under one title which a popular hymn has made familiar to us, as the sacrament of peace. More especially, because only next month the Eucharistic Congress is to take place in a country of our own speech, and one separated from us only by a few miles of sea; a country from which many of us trace, at least in part, our parentage, to which all of us owe, at least in part, the preservation of the faith in these islands. And the Eucharistic Congress, although its first object is to kindle the devotion of the faithful towards the divine mysteries, has this incidental quality—that it is the only assemblage of Catholic people from every corner of the world which takes place at fixed intervals under the patronage of a Legate from the Holy See. For one brief week the city so honoured, whether it be Sydney, or Chicago, or Dublin, becomes an image on earth of that heavenly city which the apostle saw in his vision: "the glory of God hath enlightened it, and the Lamb is the lamp thereof; and the nations shall walk in the light of it, and the kings of the earth shall bring their glory and honour into it" (Apoc. 21:23). The nations, the kings of the earth; there, rather than at Geneva, rather than at Ottawa, is the centre of the world for the time being, and the focus of the world's peace.

"Peace I leave with you; my peace I give unto you; not as the world giveth, give I unto you" (John 15:27)—that is our Lord's promise. How is it that the world gives us peace, or tries to give us peace; and why is that effort unsatisfying? Partly, of course,

Sacrament Most Holy

because peace in the true sense, in the Christian sense, is a threefold gift, and the world only offers us one-third of it. True peace means peace with God, peace within ourselves, and peace with one another. I think it is probably true that the world at this moment is more genuinely anxious for the maintenance of peace between nations than it has ever been in all its history; nor should we do well to belittle or to deride the efforts made, even by those who differ deeply from us in fundamental opinions, to secure an object so dear to the heart of Christ. But, if the last irrevocable treaty were signed, and the last cruiser scrapped, and the last gun melted down, would that be peace? Peace in a world that for the most part either forgets God, or openly defies him? Peace in a world where human hearts, emancipating themselves from every moral tie, are carried to and fro by their passions, and win from the gratification of them only discontent? For the war within our own intellects, for the war within our own wills, the world has no solution to offer; hold congresses at every town in Switzerland, and our hearts will still be a battleground, for God made them for himself, and they can find no rest until they find rest in him.

But that is not the whole difficulty. Even when it offers us peace between nations, the world is uncertain whether it will be able to implement its promises, because its present mood is only the mood of an age, and it will pass. I do not doubt the sincerity of those who are working in our time for disarmament and for the increase of national goodwill. But their task is being made easy for them by factors which are not constant factors in human thought. Citizens are over-taxed, and disarmament appeals because it means less taxation. Rulers are alarmed by revolutionary movements, and revolutionary movements find their opportunity when a nation is under arms. Besides, we are still under the influence of reaction from the experiences of the last war, like men caught by the backwash of a current. All that means that at this moment we want peace; shall we be wanting peace fifty years hence? Only if we find some deeper, some stronger motive for cultivating it. And the Catholic Church, if she can rise to the opportunity that is offered, has a stronger motive to propound than any other. *Caritas Christi urget nos* (2 Cor. 5:14): the fellowship of Catholics all over the world ought to be enough to give the world peace. It has not succeeded in doing so hitherto; that is not the fault of the Church; it is our fault, the fault of Catholics who have not been Catholic enough.

You will say that world politics are on too vast a scale to engage the active loyalties of undistinguished citizens like ourselves. Be it so; let us admit that charity begins at home. Do we, even within the narrow limits of our own parish, our own neighbourhood, our own immediate circle of friends, avail ourselves of the grace offered us in this sacrament of peace; do we consider, as much as we ought to consider, whether our communions are having the effect on our lives they ought to have, in helping us to live at peace with those around us? You see, I think that is an aspect of eucharistic doctrine which was very prominent in the first age of the Church, but is nowadays very little mentioned; too little mentioned. That is not altogether surprising. When the Church was yet small, and scattered, and persecuted, there was a kind of natural freemasonry among its members which gave them a feeling of solidarity, though even then, even in the lifetime of the apostles, there were schisms and jealousies—you see St Paul trying, with a noble impatience, to extinguish

Sacrament Most Holy

them. In the Middle Ages, when Christendom still preserved a single set of traditions, and those traditions were threatened by a solid block of Mahomedan culture in the East, it was still possible to rouse the common conscience of Europe, at least in defence of the Holy Places. But in our own day, when the society in which we live is so little Catholic, so largely even un-Christian, it is not surprising if Catholic sympathies fail to find a rallying-point. The *philadelphia*, the love of the brotherhood which St Peter and St Paul preached, is not, in our day, the self-evident thing it was at the time when St Peter and St Paul preached it.

It is the teaching of the fathers, that the very elements used in the celebration of the holy mysteries are themselves symbolical of that unity which is part of their sacramental effect. A loaf of bread is so many ears of corn; they have lost their identity now, they are indistinguishable, because they have passed into the unity of a single product. A bottle of wine is the juice of so many grapes, separate once, but now merged, still more evidently than the ears of corn, into a single fluid essence. And as the offerings are, so ought the congregation to be which makes those offerings, one single whole, compact of a number of separate units. That is definitely stated in the secret prayer of today's Mass: "In thy mercy, O Lord, we beseech thee, grant to thy Church the gifts of unity and peace, which are mystically signified by the gifts we offer up." And it is the meaning, surely, of the text which I read to you just now: "We, being many, are one bread, one body, all that partake of Christ." Think of yourself as flying in an aeroplane over the great open-air Mass at the Eucharistic Congress. You mount higher and higher, and as you mount you can no longer see separate people, only groups of people; higher still, and even the groups of people begin to grow into one another; and at last, if visibility serves, you see the whole of that vast congregation as a single dark speck. That is the true view of a Catholic congregation. It is one bread, offering itself in the Mass to Christ. Representatives, maybe, of every nation under heaven; but one bread in Christ.

And when the miracle of transubstantiation has happened, then not less but more the sacred elements become a sacrament to us of our common union in Christ. For here, beyond the furthest reach of our earth-bound imaginations, the accidents of bread and wine inhere in a substance not their own, the very substance of our Lord's body and blood. The whiteness of the bread inhering in his body; its taste, inhering in his body; its size, shape, chemical properties inhering in his body; they have all lost the old focus in which they were united, and have become united in a new focus instead, the body of Christ. Is not that to remind us, that all our natural friendships and ties and loyalties ought to be supernaturalized when we partake of this holy gift, transmuted into one single supernatural solidarity, the union of Christian people, through Christ, in Christ? Husband and wife, one now in Christ; mother and child, one now in Christ; friends, schoolfellows, neighbours, guild-members, one now in Christ.

Oughtn't we to think of that sometimes, you and I, when we go to communion? We are so accustomed to think of our communions as a transaction between our blessed Lord and our own souls, quite private, quite separate, with all the rest of the world shut off from us by the intimacy of that greeting. You are so accustomed to think of that one Host in the ciborium which you are going to receive; your

Sacrament Most Holy

Host, the one in which our Lord is waiting to give himself to you. All that is quite legitimate, quite good theology. Only, oughtn't we sometimes to remember that there is another side to it; that what is contained in the ciborium is not many Christs but one; one Christ, waiting to give himself to a whole congregation, give all of himself to each that each may be one with all? Remember, too, that when we receive the sacred Host we are receiving the blood of Christ, sharing in that true loving-cup which he shared with his disciples before he went out to drain, alone, the chalice of his agony. We all know the famous picture of St John at Ephesus, giving holy communion to our blessed Lady. When we think of that, let us remember that even such love as theirs only found its perfection when it was cemented, not with the memory of Christ dying on the cross, but by the gift of Christ living in the Holy Eucharist.

This unity is there, is real; it only remains for us to make it our own by corresponding with the grace given us, too often neglected. If we would only try to realize our membership in Christ, then perhaps, little by little, bickerings in families would begin to disappear, and then feuds in parishes, and then jealousies between parish and parish, between diocese and diocese; until at last—who knows?—nations themselves might catch the infection of the movement, and the Catholics of Europe, nay, of the whole world, would interpose themselves as a solid barrier against any disturbance of the world's peace. Certainly those of us who go to Dublin next month ought to pray, not for England only, nor for Ireland only, but for a world wanting guidance, wanting unity, wanting charity, wanting self-sacrifice. Let us pray for all the intentions commended to us lately by the tender heart of our Holy Father, so wide in its sympathies, so

RONALD KNOX

sensitive to the needs of our time; here before Jesus in the Blessed Sacrament, that his Sacred Heart, no less wide in its embrace, no less tender in its complete humanity, may weld our divided prayers together in the crucible of his divine charity, and offer them before God, a sweet-smelling sacrifice and a propitiation for the sins of the whole world.

XXII

Bread and Wine

Whatsoever the Lord pleased, he hath done in heaven and in earth.
(Ps. 134:6)

MOST OF US, I suppose, when we are celebrating some mystery of our holy religion, prefer to contemplate it simply as it presents itself to the tranquil eye of faith, and to forget, for the time being, the echoes of theological controversy and the niceties of theological definition. But I am venturing this morning to consider as briefly as I can, and to put as simply as I can, the theology of the Holy Eucharist. So much dust has been raised in the press lately, through no fault of ours, over the word transubstantiation, that we shall do well, just now, to have this doctrine clearly before our minds, and to be able, even, to present it in some sort of way if we are questioned about it by our Protestant friends.

Let us approach the subject in this way—we know something of what our Lord could do, and something of what our Lord did, from the records of his life which have been left to us in the holy gospels. And the mention of bread and wine, the elements from which the Blessed Sacrament is consecrated, naturally recalls to us two of the greatest miracles he performed while he was with us on earth, the miracle by which he changed water into wine at Cana of

RONALD KNOX

Galilee (John 2), and the miracle by which he multiplied five loaves so as to feed five thousand men beside the lake of Genesareth (John 6). Let us see what he did on those occasions, and then see whether it throws any light on what he does, day by day, through the hands of his priests, in the Blessed Sacrament of the altar.

Let's take the miracle of Cana first. Our Lord *changed* water into wine; he didn't annihilate water, and then create wine. It is, of course, within the power of almighty God both to create and to annihilate what he has created. But he didn't do that; it would have been easier, perhaps, for our limited intelligence if he had. The servants at the wedding feast didn't look down and find that the water had mysteriously disappeared from the water-pots, didn't look down a moment later, and find that the pots had suddenly filled up with wine. No, St John refers to Cana of Galilee as the place where Jesus *made* water wine; he actually altered something which was there into something else. That which had previously been water was now wine. How do you conceive that? How do you picture that to yourself?

Well, you say, now that you put it like that, it's not very easy. Let us see, how would this do? You know the old line of Crashaw, perhaps the most ingenious line in Latin poetry, *Nympha pudica Deum vidit, et erubuit*[1]—the shame-faced water saw its Lord, and blushed. The water blushed—isn't that perhaps the best way of describing it? The colour of the water was changed, so that it looked red instead of colourless. The taste of the water was changed, so that it resembled the taste of wine, and of good wine. The medical properties of the

---

1. Richard Crashaw, *Epigrammata Sacra*, "Aquae in Vinum Versae."

water changed, so that it had that power of quickening the heart's motion which belongs to fermented drink. It had, therefore, all the effects, gave, therefore, all the impression, of wine. But it was water all the same; the thing which was there after the miracle was the same thing which was there before the miracle—water; only the divine power had altered its natural properties so as to meet the needs of the situation. Yes, that would be it.

May I make two comments on that explanation you have just given? The first is that in giving it you have recognized the difference between substance and accidents. You have declared, in unphilosophical language, that in the miracle at Cana of Galilee the substance remained the same, while the accidents were changed; it was a miracle of trans-accidentation. In the second place, you have turned the miracle into a trick. It was not really wine the guests drank, it was water which had the properties of wine; and the Evangelist is wrong in speaking of the water as having *become* wine, wrong in saying that our Lord *made* water wine. No, it will not do; what happened at Cana of Galilee was a total change; the water, both in respect of its accidents and in respect of its substance, was turned into wine; became what was needed.

What happens, then, in the miracle of the Holy Eucharist? Our Lord does not do, what you expected him to do at Cana of Galilee, change both accidents and substance at once. He changes the substance without changing the accidents. He changes bread into his flesh, wine into his blood. The colour remains, and the taste, and all the physical effects and all the outward determinations of bread and wine. Just as you thought that at Cana of Galilee what the guests received was something which *was* water but had the outward properties of wine, so in the Blessed Sacrament what is received is something which has the outward properties of bread and wine, but *is* Christ. There is no trickery here, no appeal to fallacious outward appearance; on the contrary, it is our sense-experience which remains undisturbed; what is changed is the substance, that which the thing is, that which makes it what it is in the sight of the Creator who called it into existence. God, who can create and can annihilate, can also change this into that; in the Blessed Sacrament it is his will that the change should be supra-sensible, and that the substance which is truly present should be only seen, only tasted, by faith.

I must apologize if I pause for a moment to consider a criticism recently made by a bishop of the Anglican Communion. He made, if you remember, the blasphemous suggestion that a consecrated Host should be subjected to chemical analysis, to see whether it would produce any reactions different from those produced by an unconsecrated wafer. It is, of course, a curious assumption that the forms of chemical analysis known to modern Science are necessarily capable of penetrating the innermost secrets of physical reality. But I need hardly point out to you that however far Science may progress in the direction of reading that riddle, it is not possible that it should ever arrive at the point of separating accidents from their substance, since the distinction here, albeit real, is a metaphysical and not a physical distinction. Whatever tests Science proposes must necessarily report, in the long run, to our senses; such are their terms of reference. Whereas the change that takes place in transubstantiation is, as I have said, supra-sensible, and cannot submit to the award of any physical test whatever.

Sacrament Most Holy

But now, we have only mastered half our problem. The miracle of transubstantiation does not merely mean that one substance is changed into another. It is not simply that the substance of bread and wine is turned into the substance of flesh and blood. The bread is changed into a particular body, the body which was born of Mary at Bethlehem. The wine is changed not merely into blood but into the very blood which was spilt for our redemption on Calvary. How is it that an unlimited quantity of material substance—all the hosts that have ever been consecrated since the first Maundy Thursday, all the hosts that ever will be consecrated until the last judgment—can be changed into a limited quantity of material substance, the body and blood of Christ?

To get our ideas clear about that, let us turn our attention to the other miracle I mentioned, that of the five thousand. This, you will notice, is the exact correlative of the miracle at Cana of Galilee. For there both the substance and the accidents of the water were changed into those of wine; nothing remained unaltered, except the quantity of matter present. The jar which had hitherto contained two or three firkins of water now contained two or three firkins of wine, no more and no less. Whereas in the miracle of the five thousand the substance and the accidents alike remain unaltered; bread and fishes it was, bread and fishes it remains. But the quantity has changed; a moment ago it lay in a schoolboy's satchel, a morning's meal for his healthy appetite; now, five thousand men eat and are satisfied, and the fragments of the meal fill twelve baskets. In the one case there is change without multiplication; in the other multiplication without change.

Once again, then, we see what God could have done, if he had willed to do it. Just as he could have changed every host in the world into his own body, visible to our sight and sensible to our touch; so, if he would, he could have multiplied that sacred body, substance and accidents alike; so that it should suffice for every altar in the world until the end of time. But, here again, he has not done what he might have done. He has multiplied only the substance, not the accidents, of his body and blood in this sacrament—or, to speak more truly, there has been no multiplication at all. For extension in space is, as much as colour or taste or touch, one of the accidents which inhere in the substance of a thing, not part of the substance; the substance itself has no parts or magnitude, belonging as it does to the supra-sensible order. It is not *part* of the substance of our Lord's body, but the whole of it, that is conveyed by each Host in that ciborium behind me.

Our Lord, then, seems to have performed these two miracles with the special purpose of confirming our faith in the Blessed Sacrament. He would have us say to ourselves, "Yes, this is a wonderful miracle that he does in the Mass, to change the substance of bread and wine into the substance of his own body and blood, so that this body and blood is conveyed to the millions of the faithful by all the million Hosts of the world. But, after all, he did still more evident miracles while he lived amongst us, turned the substance and accidents of water into the substance and accidents of wine; multiplied the substance and accidents of five loaves of bread to feed a hungry multitude." And, since he has thus attached a kind of sacramental significance to these two particular miracles, I wonder if it is fanciful to try and read, in these miracles, a lesson about the way in which he wants his marvellous sacrament to be used, about the place he wants it to take in our lives?

Sacrament Most Holy

I should like, quite briefly, to draw your attention to three points. The first is this, that our Lord means his sacrament to be a thing for ordinary use, and also a thing for special occasions. When he fed the five thousand, he was intent on merely sustaining life; some of them certainly, though perhaps not all of them, would have fainted by the way if they had lacked this nourishment. So our Lord means the Holy Eucharist to be the constant food, and even if we will the daily food of our souls; he doesn't mean it to be *merely* a thing for great occasions. And at the same time, the miracle at Cana of Galilee is meant to show us that the Holy Eucharist is a thing for special occasions too. Our Lord did one of his two great sacramental miracles to grace a wedding feast; and every great feast, such as this, calls us to communion, and calls for a specially devout and a specially well-prepared communion.

And the second point is this, that both the miracle of the five thousand and the miracle of Cana have the same social character. A picnic in the open air, the same food handed round from each man to his neighbour—how it draws us together and makes us feel our human interdependence, our common heritage of daily toil and daily food! A wedding feast—how it diffuses, if only for the moment, the happiness of two human beings over the crowd of friends who collect to do them honour and to wish them joy! So the sacrament of Holy Eucharist is meant to have a social value—a social value to which, I am afraid, we Catholics are sometimes less alive than our Protestant neighbours. We think of receiving holy communion as a solitary act which only affects ourselves; if others are receiving it at the same time, that is only to save the priest trouble.... That is not, you know, the way in which our Lord meant us, or the way in which the Church means us, to look upon holy communion. It is a sacramental assertion of that bond of fellowship which unites all the faithful, which should unite them, alas, more closely and more sensibly than it does. As the bread is made from hundreds of ears ground in the same mill, as the wine is made from hundreds of grapes trodden in the wine-press, so we, being many, are one in Christ; we become one body among ourselves through our incorporation into him.

And one last point; both in the miracle of the five thousand and in the miracle of Cana our Lord leaves something to his human assistants. "Give ye them to eat," he says to his disciples; it is in their hands and as the result of their ministry that the wants of his people will be miraculously satisfied. "Fill the waterpots with water," he says to the servants at Cana, and they fill them up to the brim—if they had drawn less water before the miracle happened, you see, there would have been less wine at the end of it. So in this most august sacrament of his risen and ascended body and blood, although the grace of it and the honour which it does to us so far surpass all our human hopes and deserving, he does ask for our co-operation; he does invite us to correspond, by our own devotion, with the grace we receive, does reward us in proportion as he finds in our hearts those good dispositions which he asks of us. May this sacrament be the constant food of our earthly pilgrimage, and comfort our souls for their last passage through the valley of death.

XXIII

Prope Est Verbum (ROM. 10:8)

Lord, trouble not thyself, for I am not worthy that thou shouldest enter under my roof; for which cause neither did I think myself worthy to come to thee; but say the word, and my servant shall be healed. (LUKE 7:6–7)

THOSE FAMILIAR WORDS, *Domine non sum dignus*, familiar to us whenever we hear Mass or approach to receive holy communion, are worth studying in their original context. Like many of the scriptural formulas which have been enshrined in the liturgy of the Church, they tend to become staled for us by repetition; and it is well that they should recover their freshness, now and again, by being examined in the light of the occasion on which they were first spoken. There was a centurion, a Gentile, clearly, but well-disposed towards the Jewish religion, if not actually a proselyte, who had gone so far as to build a synagogue for his Jewish neighbours. We are not to think of him as some dashing young officer, the son of rich parents; he was only a sergeant, a sergeant-major at the best, not probably of very much education or of very great wealth. He had a servant who was on the point of death; and the rulers of the synagogue he had built willingly undertook to go and secure for him, in his need, the miraculous help of the new prophet who had come out of Galilee. And they besought our Lord earnestly, saying,

RONALD KNOX

"He is worthy that thou shouldest do this for him." He is worthy that thou shouldest do this for him—how typical that utterance is of the well-meaning busybodies who try to get things done in this world! "You are busy, of course, but this is really an exceptional case; he is a very useful person, and a kindness done to him might have important effects on the progress of religion in our district." Our Lord smiled, perhaps, and went with them.

And the centurion, whose worthiness has been so insisted on by his neighbours, sends a message to protest his own unworthiness. He has thought better of his original request; what right has he to monopolize, even for a moment, the attention of this prophet whom the multitudes throng to see? Lord, I am not worthy that you should come to my house; I did not even think myself worthy to come into your presence. All I ask of your charity is that you should heal my servant; you will be able to do that, surely, by a word spoken at a distance. I also, he says, am a man subject to authority, having soldiers under me, and I say to one, Go, and he goeth, and to another, Come, and he cometh, and to my servant, Do this, and he doth it. You see, our centurion has the military mind; you might almost say that he has the red-tape mind of the War Office. He is accustomed to receiving his orders from the military tribune, who receive orders from the *legatus legionis*. And the centurion, in his turn, delegates those orders to others. Is there a malefactor to be hunted down, a desert fort to be garrisoned, a party of brigands to be pursued? He does not undertake such minor duties himself; he gives a command to his inferior officers, and leaves them to carry out the commission and report. Surely it will be the same with this mysterious prophet? He has angels at his command, who will do his

Sacrament Most Holy

bidding at a word; what need, then, for his personal presence, who is so much needed elsewhere? Trouble not thyself—do not *bother*, it is a slang term he uses—just give the order, and it will be all right. We are both invested with authority; we understand one another, you and I.

Our Lord consents; rewarding, thereby, his faith, rebuking thereby the want of faith shown by those who came to plead for him. These Israelites, who ought to have known better; who must have read in their scriptures how Eliseus had cured Naaman of the leprosy without even coming downstairs to interview him (4 Kgs. 5)—they can think of no way in which health could be restored to the sick man unless our Lord can exorcize the disease by the virtue of his bodily presence. But this poor Gentile, with his rough military metaphors, his blunt, straightforward way of looking at things, has shown himself more adept at theology than they. If you talked to him about *actio in distans*, he would have no idea what you meant. But he can understand that the power which can heal all sicknesses is not tied down by conditions of time and space.

He had the faith that did not need the reassurance of actual, personal contact. That faith, as our Lord himself implied, is a rare one; and accordingly it was our Lord's habit, when he performed his miracles, not merely to perform them in person, but to reinforce the lesson of them (where it was possible) by physical contact. So we read that when he healed the deaf and dumb man he put his fingers into his ears, and spat, and touched his tongue; because words had no power to reach him, he would reassure him by a gesture. He knew how difficult it was for the hesitating soul to make an act of faith—such an act of faith as he ordinarily required from those he purposed to heal—unless it could say to itself: "He has come to me; he has come, bringing with him his miraculous powers of healing, to exercise them on me."

And if it was difficult for the men of our Lord's own day to exercise faith without physical presence and physical contact, how difficult it is for us, all these centuries afterwards, to bring our spiritual diseases to him, unless he is physically present, is physically in contact with ourselves. There are two really staggering affirmations which the Christian religion involves, compared with which all its other doctrines are easy to assimilate. One is this: God cares for everybody. And the other is this: God cares for me.

You pass through the streets as you go to your daily work, and see all those thousands of your fellow beings—faces hardened by money-getting, faces impudent with the affectation of vice, faces vacant with frivolity, faces lined with despair—and it seems to you impossible that each one of these faces, with so little recognition in it of a divine vocation or of eternal destiny, can yet represent a soul for which God cares. And yet he does care, if theology is to mean anything; cares for this one as he cares for Zacchaeus (Luke 19), cares for that one as he cared for Mary Magdalen, cares for that one as he cared for the rich young man (Matt. 19), cares for that one as he cared for the penitent thief. All these millions of human souls, and he cares for each, thirsts for each. And then suddenly you think of your own soul, only one among all those millions, and among all those millions so little distinguished by really vivid faith, by really generous love, by real intimacy with the things of eternity; can it really be, you ask yourself, that he cares for me? Just that little circle of friends he had while he lived on earth, just that handful of Jews,

Sacrament Most Holy

his fellow countrymen; for them, perhaps, he did care, did think of them when he prayed on the mountain-side or agonized in Gethsemani. But did that human regard of his extend now to all the souls existing now, all those millions, and among those millions does it extend to me?

That is the doubt, the scruple, which the Blessed Sacrament sets aside for us. The Blessed Sacrament, in the perpetuity of its institution and in the universality of its application, visualizes for us, makes imaginable for us, the perpetuity and the universality of the divine love. It was not enough for our Lord that he should become incarnate as man, that the whole fullness of the Godhead should dwell in a human form, should become, for a time, a little baby on a human mother's breast. That the God who made all things and upholds all things by the word of his power should become part of his own creation, should confine himself within the conditions of time and space, for our sakes, so as to bring himself close to us, put himself within our reach—that was not enough. If he was to live the life of an ordinary man, he must be like all other natural objects present only in one place, absent from all other points in space; his immediate presence must be confined and his immediate attention must be concentrated on a particular set of people; that would not do. And again, if he was to live the life of an ordinary man, that life must come to an end; his presence on earth would be limited to a particular period of history. It would be possible for the blind man by the roadside to hear from the multitudes the joyful tidings, "Jesus of Nazareth passes by"; but it would only be possible for one or two blind men here and there, within one limited orbit of the world's circumference; and moreover, at one definite period in history, never again. We, living nineteen centuries after the time of the emperor Tiberius, living far away at the end of the next Continent, should never be able to cry, "Jesus of Nazareth passes by," in our turn. The merciful effects of the Incarnation might be applied to the needs of our souls, but we should never be able to feel, in this life, that the Son of God had come close to us too, so far away, so many centuries later. To kindle our love with any consciousness of his near presence, the Incarnation was not enough.

To secure that further object, the Incarnation of our Lord was at once perpetuated and universalized in the sacrament of the Holy Eucharist. Wherever there was a priest to celebrate the holy mysteries, there should be Bethlehem, and there Calvary. The ciborium and the monstrance should be for us to the last end of time that manger in the stable where Christ was born, that home whither he bade his first disciples come to see where he dwelt, that boat which bore him across the lake of Galilee, that tomb where he was buried, that cenacle where he showed himself glorified; everywhere and at all times it should be possible for men to say, "Christ is here." With a prouder boast than the Jews of old, Christians should be able to cry out, "What other nation is there so great, that hath its God approaching so near to it?" (Deut. 4:7). Oh see, within a creature's hand the vast Creator deigns to be, reposing infant-like as though on Joseph's arm, or Mary's knee[1]—all that we should be able to say, as we gathered around the tabernacle and saw the monstrance lifted above our heads.

But even that was not enough. If that had been all, if there had

---

1. From Fr Faber's Hymn to the Blessed Sacrament, "Jesus, my Lord, my God, my All."

Sacrament Most Holy

been Mass, and Benediction, and processions of the Blessed Sacrament, we should be able to say, "See how near *our* God *is* to us," but we should not be able to say, "See how near *my* God is to *me*." And because he cares for each of us, not merely for all of us as a body, but for each of us as a lonely individual soul, he devised for us this still more merciful dispensation—he would come to us, singling us out for his visitation, in holy communion. When almighty God perpetuated the mystery of the Incarnation in the mystery of the Holy Eucharist, then his love radiated outwards, like the ripples that spread themselves from edge to edge of a sheet of calm water when a stone has been thrown into the middle of it. But when he saw fit to localize and individualize this mystery of the Holy Eucharist in the mystery of communion, then his love soared over us, like an eagle that sweeps down in narrower and ever narrower circles above its prey, searching for and singling out your soul and mine for the bestowal of its gifts. He comes close to us, gives himself to us, incorporates himself with us, makes himself part of us in order that we may make ourselves part of him; the divine Lover will be content with nothing less than that.

Your Host, the Host you received this morning—in that disc of matter the miracle of transubstantiation was performed, just for you. He came and dwelt there, just for you; as the whole of the sun's glorious face is repeated in every puddle by the roadside, so in every single consecrated Host the whole substance of Christ's glorified body subsists, and with it his soul and his divinity; when a hundred Hosts are consecrated, it is not one miracle that is performed, but a hundred miracles; and one was for you. When you realize that admirable condescension, that God made that one piece of bread become his own body and blood for your sake, then, perhaps, you will shrink back, and cry out with the centurion: "No, no, not that! I am not worthy that thou shouldest come under my roof, I who am only a creature, only one among so many million of creatures, and that one so marred by imperfections, so stained with sin. A countless host of angels waits about thy throne, speeds this way and that to do thy bidding; send one of these, Lord, to give me the grace I need for this day, the strength I need to conquer these temptations; do not trouble thyself, Master, to come to me."

But he will not have that, now. "I will come and heal him," that is the method which, infinitely condescending, he has decreed for our sanctification. No secondary agent, no intermediary, shall communicate to us the influence our souls need; he will come to us himself. How he must love us, to want to do that! How resolute he must be that nothing on his side should be wanting, that no loophole of excuse should be given us for refusing what he offers, when he brings it us himself! And we so blind, we so hesitating, we so neglectful; we so unwilling to give ourselves wholly to him who thus gives himself wholly to us! May he triumph over our unworthiness, and over those faint-hearted scruples that make an excuse of our unworthiness, come into our souls and overmaster them and transform them into his likeness and incorporate them utterly with himself, that henceforth we may live no more, but he in us, the food, the health, the energy of our souls.

XXIV

Novum Pascha Novae Legis

Lord, give us always this bread. (JOHN 6:34)

IT IS IMPOSSIBLE for Christian people to read the story of that miracle by which our Lord multiplied five loaves to feed five thousand people without being reminded of the Blessed Sacrament. But it is well that we should remind ourselves precisely what is the relation between the miracle and the sacrament. You will find rationalist critics today, who, in their eagerness to discredit the whole supernatural element in the gospels, will tell you that the story of the five thousand is nothing more or less than that of a sacrament which has been falsely represented as a miracle. Our Lord, they will tell you, taking his five thousand followers apart, initiated them into the mystery of a sacrificial meal, dividing up five loaves among the multitude in a symbolic manner; and the story grew up afterwards—of course, it was only a mistake—that the tiny morsels of bread which these communicants received had been endowed with supernatural efficacy to satisfy their bodily hunger. Now, that idea that the feeding of the five thousand was a sacrament, not a miracle, is doubly false. The event is recorded in all four Evangelists, and in each of them,

---

Title taken from the Sequence of the Mass of Corpus Christi, *Lauda Sion*.

even in St John, it is the miraculous element in the story that is emphasized above all else. It is hard to see why we should have been told about the twelve baskets of fragments otherwise. And meanwhile, no evangelist suggests that the meal in question had any sort of sacramental character; all alike take it for granted that the primary purpose of the miracle was to satisfy a common physical need.

It was a miracle, not a sacrament, and yet it was a miracle which was designed to prepare the way for a sacrament, and make the difficulties of sacramental doctrine easier for our weak faith. There are two mysteries above all that stagger human belief in the doctrine of the Holy Eucharist. One is that something can be changed into something else; that bread can become flesh, and wine can become blood. The other is that the human flesh and blood which Christ took from his blessed Mother can be multiplied so as to feed, day by day, millions of the faithful. And in either case our Lord has given us something much better than an explanation, he has given us proof. Do you find it difficult, he says, to believe that the wine in the chalice becomes my blood, through a change which affects its substance? See me, then, at Cana of Galilee, change not the substance only of water, but substance and accidents together, water itself, into wine! Do you find it difficult to believe that my one human body can, by the multiplication of its substance, become present in all the myriad hosts of the world? Then see me, by the Lake of Galilee, multiply not the substance only of bread, but substance and accidents together, bread itself, until five thousand people eat of five loaves, and are satisfied! In either case, he proves by a visible miracle his power to work that invisible miracle which will take place in this church half an hour from now.

Sacrament Most Holy

But this miracle had a further educative value. It marked at once the resemblances and the differences between the old covenant, the covenant which almighty God made with the Jews, and the new covenant which came into force with the Christian Church. Under the old dispensation, God chose out for himself an Assembly—or a Church, it is all the same word—to be his chosen people. He led them for long years through a wilderness till at last they arrived at Canaan, the promised land. Under the new dispensation he chose out for himself a Church—or an Assembly, it is all the same word— and promised to lead them through the wilderness of this transitory world into the rest which he had prepared for them beyond the gates of death. His old people, the Jews, needed material food on their material pilgrimage through the desert (Exod. 16:31–35); he gave them manna from heaven. His new people, the Christian Church, will need spiritual food on its spiritual pilgrimage; he gives it that bread from heaven which is his own body.

The miracle of the five thousand, then, is an intermediate stage between the gift of manna in the wilderness and the gift of our Lord's own body and blood in the Holy Eucharist. It is to correct the ideas which these Jewish followers of his have formed as to what they are to expect when they pray for heavenly food. As a more perfect type of the Blessed Sacrament, the multiplication of bread for the five thousand is at once compared with, and contrasted with the gift of manna to the Israelites. Let me give you three points which bring out the comparison, and three points which bring out the contrast.

First, then, for the comparison. The manna in the wilderness was given to be food for the wilderness, and to be daily food. During forty years, the supply of manna never failed, but during all that time it had to be gathered daily, it must not be laid aside and kept. So here in the wilderness beyond the sea of Galilee, our Lord gives the multitude only what they need to support them in the wilderness; they take nothing home with them. And in the same way the Holy Eucharist is the daily bread of our pilgrimage. When we have passed through the gates of death and reached, please God, the land of our expectation, we shall have no more need of signs and sacraments; there is no need for communion in heaven. But until that time, the Holy Eucharist may be, if we will, should be, if we have the opportunity, our daily food; renewing in us from day to day the image of our Lord's charity. The day's food for the day's march—that is what holy communion is meant to be.

Next, in the story of the miracle you must notice the words "they did *all* eat." It was a common meal for our Lord's followers—five thousand of them this time, only four thousand a little later, when (as St John tells us) many of his disciples left him because they could not understand his doctrine. It is a common meal, to partake of it is a sign of membership. Under the old covenant, to partake of the manna was a bond which united those pilgrims in the wilderness: "they did all eat," says St Paul, "the same spiritual food." And for us Christians the Holy Eucharist is a bond which at once attests and promotes our Christian unity. As the one loaf of bread is ground from so many different ears of corn, so we, individuals distinct from one another, become one body when we receive holy communion, incorporated into Jesus Christ. To be a partaker of the one altar is the test, the pledge, the bond of our Christian fellowship.

They did all eat, the Gospel says, and were filled. And the disciples, we are told, distributed to them "as much as they would."

Sacrament Most Holy

So it was with the children of Israel in the desert; they did not take up, each of them, the same amount; each man took up an amount exactly proportioned to the needs of his household. "They gathered one more, another less: neither had he more that had gathered more, nor did he find less that had provided less"; under the divine direction, each man satisfied his own needs, and satisfied them exactly. The same, surely, is true of the spiritual nourishment which we derive from the Holy Eucharist. The same sacred Host which will support an ordinary workaday Christian like you and me through the dull, daily round of his lukewarm pieties would suffice, if a saint received it instead, to inspire his incessant prayer, his heroic mortifications. God gives his grace in fullest measure where he finds empty vessels to receive it. All ate and all were filled, but each was filled in proportion as he hungered for the food given him—so it is, day by day, at the communion rails.

The day's food for the day's march, the bond of fellowship, sufficiency proportioned to the needs of each—such was the manna in the desert, such was the bread miraculously multiplied, such is the gift which we receive in holy communion. And now for the contrast. The Israelites in the wilderness found the manna, indeed, lying close about their encampment, but still they must go out and gather it by their own exertions. So, when the multitudes were hungry after they had listened to our Lord's preaching, the apostles would have had them shift for themselves: "Send them away, that going into the next villages and towns, they may buy themselves food to eat." Our Lord will not consent to that: "Give *you* them to eat." He is making provision, surely, for the administration of his great sacrament; under the new covenant grace shall be brought to our very doors. Measure, Christians, the effort which it costs you to frequent the altar by comparison with the worth of that gift, or with the condescension which bestows it; and will you not be ashamed of the little generosity shown on your part? "I am the Lord God; open thy mouth wide, and I will fill it" (Ps. 53:11).

And yet at the same time there is this difference; under the old dispensation man could do nothing for himself, must remain a mere pensioner on the divine goodness, contributing nothing to his own support. Man restored by grace under the new dispensation is dignified with the privilege of offering something to God as well as receiving from him. "Give you them to eat." True enough that all we can do is infinitely little; whence can a man provide bread, here in the wilderness? And yet there is something we can do: "How many loaves have you?" Only very little we can do, but it is something, and that something God condescends to want. Just five loaves, stored away by an anxious mother in a schoolboy's satchel; that was all the human help our Lord asked when he fed the five thousand; but it was something. So, in the sacrament of his body and blood, our Lord does ask us to provide something, only common, material things, only his everyday gifts of bread and wine, but we are to contribute our human share to his banquet. And so it is with the sacramental effects of the Holy Eucharist; it is not meant, like baptism, to create good dispositions in us; rather to multiply and transform the trembling faith, the lukewarm charity it finds there. Whence shall we—whence? Why, from the little we have; he will do the rest.

And finally, one more contrast—under the new dispensation the miracle does not stop short with the bare satisfaction of our needs; grace overflows its measure. The manna, if the children of Israel did not make use of it, melted with the noonday sun; it is not so in Galilee. "Gather up the fragments that remain, lest they be lost. They gathered up therefore and filled twelve baskets with the fragments." So in the sacrament of Holy Eucharist, although it would far exceed all our deserts if he only gave himself to be our food, our Lord will redouble his condescension by remaining with us, to be adored in the monstrance or in the tabernacle; he is not content to satisfy our hunger, he spoils us, whenever we address our prayers at the altar, with the crumbs of his grace. O princely benefactor, whose very gleanings are a harvest! May he, who so mercifully sustains us on our pilgrimage with that heavenly food which is his body broken and his blood shed for us, bring us safely to his land of promise, where we shall see him no longer under sacramental veils, but face to face, satisfied with the plenteousness of his house for ever.

CHAPTER I

The Great Supper

And the Lord said to the servant: Go out into the highways and hedges, and compel them to come in. (LUKE 14:23)

THE PARABLE from which these words are taken seems either to have been used, with certain changes of detail, upon two separate occasions, or else to have been a long parable of which two different summaries have been preserved to us. It does not matter much which of those two explanations is the true one; it is certain that by comparing the story of the marriage-feast in St Matthew (Matt. 22) with the story of the great supper in St Luke we can get a composite picture which contains no element of inconsistency. A man of wealth made a great supper; think of him if you will as a king who was celebrating the occasion of his son's wedding. The first invitation was accepted—the parable clearly implies it—by a number of guests, and the preparations were made accordingly. It was only when the actual summons came, telling of the day and hour, to guests who had already accepted the invitation, that they began to change their minds. They treated the servants who brought the message with a treasonable discourtesy, and excused themselves from attendance on a variety of different grounds; a variety of excuses, but all alike failed at the last moment to avail themselves of

Sacrament Most Holy

the opportunity. The fatlings and the beeves are killed and in readiness; the preparations for the banquet are complete, only—only there are no guests. Nothing but rows of empty tables in response to the king's summons. What is to be done? There is nothing for it but to send out into the streets and lanes of the city, the highways and hedges of the countryside, and bring in the poor, the lame, the halt, and the blind, and fill up the vacant seats with guests less favoured, guests who cannot afford to refuse such generosity.

It is not difficult to see, it cannot, even when the parable was first uttered, have been difficult to see, what our Lord was hinting at. The guests who first accept the invitation, and then disappoint their host at the last moment—who can they be but the Jews, the Pharisees in particular, to whom our Lord is speaking? God has planned a great banquet for them—all the spiritual riches of the Church, if they will have them. And that banquet is also a wedding feast; for its origin and its inspiration is that ineffable union between God's nature and man's which took place at the Incarnation. That hope of redemption the Jewish people have made their own; they have looked forward to it through long centuries of unique and providential history. And now the moment of destiny has arrived; the preaching of our Lord and his apostles tells them that all things are now ready; the Church of the new covenant waits for them; they have only to come. And the invited guests revoke the acceptance they have given. Worldliness, in one form or another, has killed their appetite for the celestial delicacies so long promised to them, and with one consent they begin to make excuse. What remains to be done? What remains, but that almighty God should send out his neglected summons to the Gentile world instead, and recall the Gentiles, poor, blind, crippled, after all those centuries of wandering away from him, to enter into the inheritance which his own chosen people has refused?

The highways and the hedges, the streets and lanes of the city, the poor and the lame and the blind—that means you and me. Who were we, what were we, as God foresaw our lives in his inscrutable providence, that he should call us into the fellowship of his holy Catholic Church? There was no thing in ourselves that could attract him; there was no claim we could make upon his consideration; there was no added glory that our homage or our gratitude could bring to him, our Creator; we were creatures, and fallen. It was not simply that we were homeless, ever since we were banished from our appointed Paradise; we were helpless too, groping in the dark with limbs that could scarcely carry us. His creatures, and his fallen creatures, God called us to himself; in utter condescension, in generosity for which we can never make return. He has made us children of his Church, and has set before us a banquet of spiritual delights, which is also a marriage-feast.

Picture to yourself the rows of hungry tramps and beggars and pavement-artists, mystified, whirled off their feet, by the sudden imperious invitation, yet with no choice left to them—compelled to come in, as they range themselves about the rich man's supper-table. Twenty minutes ago, a soup-kitchen would have seemed a Paradise to them; they would have picked a crust of bread out of the gutter; and now they are sitting down before splendid dishes, at tables loaded with the things they have never seen except in shop windows. It is the Embankment turned loose at the Guildhall. That means you and me, when we go to communion. *O res mirabilis,*

Sacrament Most Holy

manducat Dominum pauper, servus, et humilis![1] Earth-born creatures, with no rights or titles of our own; sold into slavery by the sin that was our undoing, and, though ransomed by grace, still miserably poor, destitute of all spiritual resources we can call our own—what do we ask for? Grace just to keep us going. What comes to us in return? Grace that can make saints of us, if we will. We went out into the streets to look for a meal, and we were swept out of the streets into a banquet. And more than a banquet—a marriage-feast. For as, by the Incarnation, the Church becomes the mystical bride of Christ; so in the sacrament of holy communion the Christian soul is espoused to Christ. That which she desired, she holds in her embrace. For, whatever be our worldliness, all our hunger, did we but know it, is for nothing less than God; and nothing less than God is given to us when we receive the nourishment of our souls.

"They went their way, one to his farm, and another to his merchandise.... I have bought a piece of ground, I have bought a yoke of oxen, I pray thee hold me excused.... I have married a wife, and therefore I cannot come." Still, all around us, those voices are to be heard: the world's children, in their fancied security, their fancied self-sufficiency, delighting in the latest toy, the latest acquisition, find themselves too busy to accept the invitation of God's holy Church. Let us not think of them today, as we meet, children of the Catholic Church, around our family table and give thanks for this, our intimate food. But what if we, to whom daily opportunity is given of satisfying our spiritual appetite, of gratifying our souls' longing for God, make excuses in our turn; if we, spell-bound by

---
1. From the hymn of St Thomas Aquinas, "Sacris Solemniis."

our trumpery occupations, hear God's invitation to the sacrament of his body and blood, and ask him to hold us excused? Is not that as if the beggars in the hedgerows and at the street corners were to refuse the call to the king's supper—refuse it, for other aims whose worthlessness we acknowledge? What if the tramps in the parable had made their excuses too? That is what we do, if we absent ourselves from the marriage-supper of Christ.

And yet, there is something worse than that. Only in St Matthew do we find the terrible sequel to the story—how one of the guests came in without troubling to put on the wedding-garment that had been provided for him, and was found so by the king as he came to visit his guests, and at once cast into the outer darkness. It's a very odd postscript, this, to the story. Our Lord's parables are sometimes concerned with individual people, sometimes with whole groups of people; this is the only instance I know in which one of his parables begins with groups of people and then suddenly comes down to an individual. We should have expected to find that a whole section of the beggars had come in without their wedding-garments; instead, it is only one man—one man; why is that?

I don't know if it is just a fancy, but the explanation which I always suspect is that there was one man among our Lord's audience to whose conscience he wished to make a special and a last appeal. Judas Iscariot, although he had not yet betaken himself to the chief priests and made his infamous bargain, was, it may well be, already a traitor in heart; at least his future treachery was already known to him who knew all things. In a few days, he was to sit at the supper-table with the Master he was pledged to betray; most probably he was actually to receive, with that black purpose in his heart, that very body and blood which he had sold for thirty pieces of silver. Called by grace not only to be a member, but to be an apostle of the Church, he had already lost, or was soon to lose, the wedding-garment of charity which the Bridegroom's own hands had given him. A last warning, to bring him to his knees, if he will, before it is too late—surely that is how Judas must have heard the story. "Confess, Judas! Confess now, while there is still time! He has seen your heart already; he is only waiting for your confidence." That is the voice which Judas hears, and hearing does not heed.

Only one among all the guests in the story; please God, it is not often that the table of Christ is profaned by a sacrilegious communion. But when it is so profaned; when, for some unworthy end, the sinner who knows himself to be in mortal sin dares to partake of the marriage-feast, then he makes the choice of Judas and deserves Judas' punishment. Let him not console himself with comfortable Protestant doctrines about the nature of our Lord's presence in the Holy Eucharist; he knows better in his heart. He knows that the very body born of Mary, the very blood spilt on Calvary, are there; that he, who comes to the faithful as their food and their victim, comes to the sinner as his judge. The King passes down between the rows of his guests; his eye is all-penetrating, the guilty wretch cannot hide his nakedness or make answer to his condemnation; speechless, he goes out with Judas into the darkness he has made his own.

Let us thank God, then, on this glorious feast of Corpus Domini, for the unearned generosity with which he has called us to himself, for the abounding riches of what he gives us in this sacrament, for the amazing condescension of the manner in which that gift is bestowed. And let us offer reparation to him, with full hearts, for all the outrages and indignities by which his sacramental presence is profaned, wittingly or unwittingly, by the careless or by the impious; and pray that everywhere his Sacred Heart may be praised, adored, and loved in the holy sacrament of the altar until the last end of time.

You especially, who are of this congregation, should be eager thus to honour the sacred mysteries. Other parishes have some patron saint to honour, some other mystery to commemorate; your Patron is the prisoner of the tabernacle. Other parishes have relics to carry in procession, dead members of the body their saint once wore in life; your reliquary is the monstrance, your relic the living body of our Saviour Jesus Christ. You then, who worship in this church, ought to be a special guard of honour to the Blessed Sacrament; in this church, visits ought to be more frequent, Masses better attended, communions more fervent than in any neighbouring parish; yours is a royal borough. God bless the priests who minister and you who worship here, and make you abound more and more in love and gratitude for his unspeakable gift.

XXVI

A Priest for Ever

I am with you all days. (MATT. 28:20)

SET BEFORE YOUR MINDS, as you have seen it in a hundred pictures, on a hundred pious cards, the figure of Jesus Christ holding the sacred Host and the chalice in his hands. Think, for a moment, of the paradox which that involves—the figure of our Lord at the Last Supper. You see before you what seems to be the form of a man; that man is Jesus Christ, his body, his blood, his manhood, his divinity. You also see before you what seems to represent a round disc of bread. That which looks like bread is also Jesus Christ, his body, his blood, his manhood, his divinity. Jesus Christ, then, holds himself in his hands. Host and banquet, priest and victim, are one.

There's more to it than that. We are accustomed to think of the body and blood of Christ as we receive it in holy communion, not merely as the body and blood that drew life from Mary, but as the body broken and the blood shed for us on Calvary. Now, in that first communion which our Lord gave to his apostles on the first Maundy Thursday, he gave to them the same precious gift, exactly the same, as he gave to us this morning. Yet, when he stood in the upper room, and broke the bread and divided the cup among the friends from whom he was parting, the sacrifice of Calvary had not yet happened. The bread of angels has not yet been ground in the mill, the wine of salvation has not yet been trodden in the winepress, yet here, in the first Eucharist, that bread and that cup are being blessed, and received, and desecrated. The whole Christ gives the whole Christ; the living Christ gives the living Christ; the victim who has not yet been immolated gives the victim that already avails. *O admirabile commercium!*[1]

What does that mean, except that the sacrifice of Christ, although it was effected in the world of sense and under the conditions of time, is yet in its own nature spiritual and eternal? As the merits of that sacrifice could avail to deliver our Lady from all taint of sin at the instant of her conception, so they could avail to effect the miracle of transubstantiation before the sacrifice itself was enacted. And if the merits of his death lived already, before he died, how much more easily do we understand that they live on now, after his resurrection! The crucifixion happened at a particular moment in time; the pain of Calvary, the humiliation of Calvary, the agony of Calvary have ceased. It is never repeated, but that is because it has no need to be repeated; it continues, it lives. Every time a priest goes to the altar—he continues the sacrifice which Christ offered in the hour of his Passion.

The priest continues it—or rather, Christ continues it through his priest. It was not only at the Last Supper that our Lord in person gave his own body and blood with his own hands. In the Passion itself he is, all the time, the principal agent; he was offered because

---

1. Opening words of the antiphon for the *Magnificat* (Vespers, Feast of the Circumcision).

he willed it. He neglected his own opportunities for defence at his trial; he consented to carry his own cross, co-operating, as it were, in the greatest injustice of history; while he hung on the cross, the angel legions were about him, hand on scabbard, ready to interfere and to rescue him, but he waved them back; and at the last, when he laid down his life, he laid it down of his own will, at a moment of his own choosing; no man could take his life from him, he laid it down. Always, *Christus Patiens* is also *Christus Agens*: always, Christ the victim is also Christ the priest. And wherever the bloodless sacrifice is offered in the whole world, whenever the bloodless sacrifice is offered to the last end of time, it is Christ continuing on earth the work he began on earth, our reconciliation with the Father. He lies upon the altar, as he lay stretched out on the cross on Good Friday. Yet he stands at the altar, as he stood in the upper room on Holy Thursday. Operating through the consecrated hands of his unworthy priest, Christ himself blesses the bread and transforms it, and breaks, and offers, and distributes that which he has transformed.

But in the Blessed Sacrament we have more than a continuation of what happened on Maundy Thursday, more than a continuation of what happened on Good Friday: it is a continuation of our Lord's whole life. He came into the world for three ends, to be, to suffer, and to do. To be amongst us men, to make us, through his participation in our nature, participators in his, to bring heaven down to earth, Emmanuel, God with us—that is already something. And it is that divine condescension which is manifested to us in the thirty years of our Lord's hidden life, and most characteristically in the manger at Bethlehem. To suffer for men: to take upon himself, as the head of our fallen race, the sins that we could not expiate; to offer a divine victim in satisfaction to the divine justice; that was more. And it is that divine humiliation which is manifested to us in the whole of our Lord's Passion, and most characteristically on the cross of Calvary. To go about amongst men doing good: to heal the sick, give sight to the blind, to cast out the evil spirits, to raise the dead; to comfort the mourner and to rescue the souls lost in sin—that was to set the crown on the mercy of his Incarnation. And it is that divine fecundity of charity which is manifested to us in the three years of the ministry, wherever his feet trod, whenever human needs claimed and human hearts welcomed him.

And each of those three ends of our Lord's Incarnation has its analogue in the theology of the Eucharist. The Blessed Sacrament itself is the continuation of Bethlehem, is an eternal Nativity. As the Word was made flesh at the Incarnation, so that he might pitch his tabernacle amongst men, so in the mere consecration of the Holy Eucharist bread is made flesh, made that same flesh, in order that his tabernacle may remain among us to the end of time. The Holy Mass is the continuation of Calvary; as he pleaded before the Father in the days of his humiliation for the forgiveness of our sins, so now, glorified, yet under the veil of humble appearances, he pleads. And when holy communion is administered to the faithful, it is the continuation of that long and laborious ministry through which the Son of Man went about to do good. His feet cannot tire now, as they tired on the roads of Galilee; his spirit cannot glow with human anger or melt into human tears. But still, as he goes about in the person of his priest administering to the faithful, through his own body and blood, the virtue that can only come from him;

Sacrament Most Holy

giving strength to our weakness, sight to our blindness, vigour and life to our dead devotion, his earthly ministry goes on.

First, then, the Blessed Sacrament, in the tabernacle or in the monstrance, is the continuation of Bethlehem. Still, as in the days when he lived retired with Mary and his foster-father, he delights to lie hidden; only faith can penetrate the veils that surround him. As once the human form that belonged to his human nature shrouded his Godhead, so now Godhead and manhood alike are shrouded under the forms of common things. As once he waited in the stable of a wayside inn for souls enlightened by faith to come and do him homage, so now in back streets and behind cloistered doorways you will find admission to his presence. And as he waited, not only for the adoration of his servants, but for the jeers and the blasphemies of his persecutors, so now in his sacramental presence he is patient of outrage and of sacrilege—outrage deliberate or indeliberate, our carelessness in church, our indevout communions, among the rest. For his delight is to be with the sons of men; those thirty-three years he spent as man in our midst were not a prodigy, isolated and apart; rather they were the characteristic expression in time and in history of the eternal charity that *will* draw near to us, *will* rule in men's hearts, though it be to rule amongst his enemies, *will* come to his own, though his own do not receive him. And as the Incarnation is the historical expression of that eternal tendency, so the Holy Eucharist is its sacramental expression. Let it not be thought strange or unworthy that bread and wine, mute and material things, should be the vehicle of such grace. The condescension lies not in that, but in his willingness to come and meet us at all on our own ground, Creator revealing himself to creature through the creature's medium of sense. That was the beginning of his condescension, when he became man; it is only the proper and (if we may so take Love for granted) the natural continuation of that beginning, when "within a creature's hand the vast Creator deigns to be, reposing infant-like, as though on Joseph's arm or Mary's knee"[2]—Emmanuel, God with us.

But our Lord did not come to earth simply in order to *exist* as Man. There was an end for his existence as man, and that end to suffer and to be sacrificed. The Atonement is the primary purpose of the Incarnation; the road that begins at Bethlehem leads to Calvary. So in his chief sacrament our Lord becomes present, not simply for the sake of being present, but in order that being present he may be offered up. In what sense? How can the Mass be a sacrifice, if Calvary is a sacrifice complete for all time? Only once the agony and the betrayal, only once the scourging and the injustice, only once the nails, and the crown, and the spear. One drop of that blood spilt might have saved the world from all its transgressions, how much more that long pageant of pain! "And now the matchless deed's achieved, determined, dared, and done"[3]—anything else, surely, that goes by the name of sacrifice must be no more than a shadow and a pale reflex of this!

But no. Mystically, yet none the less really, the immolation as well as the oblation of the spotless Victim takes place whenever the priest goes to the altar. It is not repeated, it is continued. Though in

---

2. From Fr William Faber's Hymn to the Blessed Sacrament, "Jesus, my Lord, my God, my All."
3. Christopher Smart, "A Song to David."

Sacrament Most Holy

his own nature he be immortal, immutable, impassible, our Lord is still from day to day mystically born and slain and offered; and every such offering has in itself an infinite satisfactory value, won by that sacrifice of Calvary from which it derives. Not a repetition, but a continuation. We might use, very roughly, this analogy to bring the matter clearly before our minds. A piece of music, written years ago, was a complete work of art when the composer's hand left, once for all, the paper on which it was copied. Yet, year by year and day by day, those same harmonies are awaked whenever the piece of music is performed. Each performance is not a repetition, but a continuation of that single act by which the composer first brought it into being. So the Mass does not add to Calvary, does not multiply Calvary; it is Calvary, sacramentally multiplied. And in it, the true priest is still our Lord himself, though he makes use of a human agent to repeat the mystic words and to perform the sacramental gestures. The Mass is not the priest doing what Christ did; it is Christ continuing what Christ began.

Our Lord came to be and to suffer; he also came to do. He went about doing good. When we receive communion, we are made partakers of that same virtue which flowed from the incarnate Christ. We are reminded of that every time we go to communion by the words the priest says when he holds up the Host to our view. "Lord, I am not worthy that thou shouldst enter under my roof, but speak the word only, and my soul shall be healed." They are an echo of the words of that centurion who came to ask help from our Lord when his servant lay sick to death (Luke 7:6). "I will come and heal him" is our Lord's answer, and the centurion expostulates; cannot the word that will bring healing be spoken from afar? What need of a visible presence or a personal contact to effect the mighty works of the Omnipotent? But the common practice of our Lord in his miracles is a continuous rebuke to that attitude. He will go to find the sufferer, he will touch, he will anoint, he will speak to him—why? Because he chooses so to condescend to our service. He could have healed the sick, cleansed the leper, raised the dead, without coming to earth at all; yet he came to earth to do it. He could communicate the grace which we receive through his body and blood without any sacramental medium; yet he makes himself present on our altars to do it. Is not this a God to serve?

Are we therefore going to say to ourselves every Easter: "There, that's all right for another year"? Look back a year or two: are you going to communion now as often as you did then? Jesus Christ offers himself to you as he did a year ago, two years ago. He has no less love for you, and you, believe me, have no less need of him. Your soul is no less than it was the object of his burning zeal: claims it no less, although it deserves it no more. Can it be that he has remained constant, and you have changed? That he means less to you, not because his loving gifts are fewer now, but because you are slower to make use of them? Every morning there's a ciborium in the tabernacle, with so many Hosts in it, one for each of you. Think for a moment of your Host, the one that will be given to you, if you will come for it. In that Host, Jesus Christ himself waits for you. Sometimes you may not feel, sometimes, alas, you may not be, in a fit state to receive so tremendous a gift; but...that you should be there, kneeling in your place, others going up to receive, and from some indolence, some indifference, you should leave that one Host in the ciborium! Surely that is strange?

Sacrament Most Holy

Every Benediction is Bethlehem. Every Mass is Calvary. Every communion is Christ going about to do good. "When thou dost celebrate or hear Mass, it ought to seem to thee as great, as strange, as joyful a thing as if on this very day Christ were descending into the Womb of the Virgin and becoming Man, or hanging upon the Cross, were suffering and dying for mankind's salvation."[4] It ought to seem so: does it?

---

4. *Imitation of Christ*, Book IV, ch. 2, 6.

XXVII

Words of Life

Then Jesus said to the twelve, Will you also go away?
And Simon Peter answered him, Lord, to whom shall we go?
Thou hast the words of eternal life. (JOHN 6:69)

WHEN OUR LORD fed the five thousand in the wilderness, it was, I suppose, a demonstration in force of the little Church which he had mustered round him in Galilee. Probably, in Galilee, it was the high water mark of his evangelistic success. And St John tells us in this passage that after the miracle many of his disciples went back, and walked no more with him; it was then that the ebb of his popularity began. The other gospels do not explicitly mention this fact; but you can infer it from them quite unmistakably. On the next occasion when our Lord held a rally, as we should call it, of his followers, there were only four thousand who went out with him across the lake into the desert. Four thousand instead of five thousand, a loss of twenty per cent.

That is strange, isn't it? You would have thought that after so staggering a demonstration of his command over the forces of nature, his movement would have become more, not less popular. It is St John who supplies us with the reason. After the miracle of the five thousand, our Lord's teaching became more intimate, more explicit, about the doctrine of the Holy Eucharist. He told them that the true bread from heaven was his own flesh; that he who ate of that bread should live for ever, and so on. When our Lord bestows on us great privileges, it is his custom to make great demands of us in return. And when the faith of his followers had been strengthened by seeing the most wonderful of his miracles take place before their eyes, so strengthened that you would have thought it impossible it should ever be disturbed thenceforward, he made demands upon it. He demanded belief, even then, in the doctrine of the Holy Eucharist. And that was too much for some of them. This is a hard saying, they complained; who can hear it? And they went back, and walked no more with him.

Then Jesus said to the twelve, "Will you also go away?" Our Lord never asked questions because he wanted to know the answer. He asks them whether they will be loyal to him or not; and yet the moment after he shows that he can foresee what will become of them. "Have I not chosen you twelve?" he asks. "And one of you is a devil." Judas, perhaps just then beginning the series of petty thefts that was to lead to his downfall, and flattering himself that nobody could possibly know about it; and yet our Lord sees more than that; sees the traitor's bargain, and the rope, and the suicide's end. He knows the answer; why then does he ask? He is not asking a question; he is throwing out a challenge. He is proving their loyalty, and giving them the opportunity to assert it. One by one those thousand half-hearted supporters of his have drifted away out of sight, back to the world they had left for him—conventional phrases of gratitude, perhaps, on their lips, telling him that it has all been a very interesting experience, and that they have derived a great deal of spiritual comfort from his teaching; but they are going away, they will not walk with him any more. And as he looks sadly after them, he will use their defection as a lesson to school the loyalty of his own favoured friends. Half ironically, half pathetically, he turns to them and asks: Will you also go away?

Simon Peter answered, and with him all the apostles answered: Lord, to whom shall we go? Thou hast the words of eternal life. To go away is to go somewhere else, to sit at the feet of some other teacher, to kindle with some other enthusiasm, to find some fresh orientation for our life's ambitions. How should we do that? We have been to another teacher, we have sat at the feet of John the Baptist, and he pointed us to you. We have had our youthful enthusiasms, and outlived them; one of us at least has been a Zealot, a Jewish nationalist, sworn to uphold the movement which was to deliver our country from the empire of Rome. What became of it? He learned better; learned that there was only one hope Israel waited for, the Messiah, only one deliverance it needed, deliverance from its sins. That Messiah, that Deliverer, he found in you. We have had, some of us have had, personal ambitions; tried to make a fortune for ourselves by heaping up ill-gotten gains. And then we saw that it was a thankless task, trying to lay up treasure on earth; we looked for a leader who would give us unselfish ambitions, a cause greater than ourselves to strive for, and that leader we found in you. For you, the latest of our loyalties and the final goal of our quest, we have abandoned all the things we cared for; and now would you have us go away from you? To whom shall we go? You have the words of eternal life; have they lost their charm for human ears, or we the capacity to receive them?

Sacrament Most Holy

People do go away from the Catholic Church. With the other Christianities, the line of division is perhaps not so clearly marked; there are millions of our fellow countrymen who could not tell you, simply could not tell you, whether they are in any real sense members of the Church of England. But the Catholic system, infinitely patient, infinitely gentle as it is to the consciences of waverers, has sharper edges, and people who lose direct contact with it are more tempted to react against it. You have almost certainly heard of someone, probably enough you have known someone, within the circle of your immediate acquaintance, who has fallen away from the faith which is in Christ. He married a Protestant, and his wife's family bullied him into apostasy for the sake of the children. Or he moved into some place which was far from a Catholic church, and so fell into neglect of the sacraments, and in the end drifted away altogether. Or he made a career for himself, rose in the social scale, and in leaving behind him the other associations of his early life, managed to leave his religion along with them. And the news of such a defection as that, even when there were circumstances to explain it, is—confess it—a tiny blow to your faith; a very gentle tap to test the stability of your own spiritual foundations. He always seemed such a good Catholic; was at school with you, worked side by side with you; what a dreadful thing! I hope (you say to yourself) I shall never be tempted in that way. Another's apostasy has cast a chill of loneliness over you.

If any such doubt of yourself ever creeps into your mind, then imagine, the next time you go to communion, that your Lord coming to you in the Holy Eucharist holds himself back for a moment from your lips, and asks: Wilt thou also go away? Others, whose childhood was not less sheltered by religious influences, others, whose lives seemed not less clearly marked by the traces of a heavenly guidance, have forgotten their allegiance and denied me before men; wilt thou also go away? No man knows the force of another's temptations; the doubts, the difficulties, which perplexed one soul yesterday may perplex another tomorrow; wilt thou also go away?

And the answer? The answer is the voice of Peter, the voice of the apostles, the voice of the universal Church: Lord, to whom shall we go? If we turn away from him, we must go somewhere else—where else? We can only give up his revelation for some revelation more satisfying than his. We can only abandon the Catholic Church for some spiritual home which is more of a home than the Catholic Church. We can only despise his sacraments if we are in a position to compare them with other sources of inspiration which promise more comfort in this life, more hope in the world to come. Where are we to find such a revelation, such a spiritual home, such sources of inspiration? Nowhere; there is no other system in the world which dares even to claim what the Catholic Church claims. Are we to abandon the Catholic faith for something *less* than the Catholic faith?

Do not be afraid, for a moment, to look over that giddy edge and to imagine what it would be like, for you, to lose faith in your religion. Oh, no doubt there would be a momentary satisfaction, to the more indolent part of your nature, to find an easing of that sense of struggle which we Catholics always feel, though we may feel it only at the back of our minds, living as we do in the midst of a culture which is not ours, a culture which does not understand ours. And we might, for the time being, find an outlet for our

Sacrament Most Holy

energies, a centre for our energies, a centre for our enthusiasm, in some other movement, political or philanthropic; it would carry us along with it while youth lasted, while the excitement of it lasted. But the whole structure and fabric of our life would be gone. We should have no standards to judge by, no light to walk by, no hope to live by. We see all that, and we draw back our feet, shuddering, from the edge. We cannot contemplate the thought of walking no more with Jesus. To whom shall we go? He has the words of eternal life.

But still he holds himself back from us; this Guest who comes to us in the Holy Eucharist; he has not finished, yet, with his challenge, he wants to try our loyalty still further. His friendship, we have found, is something we cannot do without. It is not the mere routine of living that would make it impossible for us, please God, to abandon our religion; it is not merely that we cling obstinately to a set of opinions because they are *our* opinions; it not a mere sentimental attachment, such as fades and dies down with the passing of the years. Habit and head and heart, they have all something to say to it; but the anchorhold of our religion is something deeper than that, something that affects the whole of us, not a part of us. If, then, the religion of Christ is something we could not do without, how is it that most of us use it so little, live it so little? Is it meant to be like a jewel so precious that, for fear of robbery, it can never see the light of day?

We are puzzled over the attitude of lapsed Catholics; oughtn't we really be more puzzled by the attitude of slack Catholics? The people who have the faith, to whom the faith, apparently, means so little? All the staggering assertions of Catholic doctrine about what the Holy Eucharist is, a real change of the substance of bread and wine into the substance of our Lord's body and blood, all that they accept. The embarrassing regulations which the Church imposes upon us, that we should go to Mass every Sunday, that we should purify our consciences and receive holy communion at Easter time, all that they comply with; or, even if they fall short of it, they admit that they are in the wrong when they do so; they are content to carry a burdened conscience. The mystery they believe, the burden they accept; but the consolations of the Holy Eucharist, the privileges conferred on us in the Holy Eucharist, seem to mean nothing to them at all. They still walk with Christ, but they walk with him, as it were, at a distance, in embarrassed silence, instead of throwing themselves upon the enjoyment of his companionship. "Did not our hearts burn within us," asks the two disciples on Easter evening, "while he talked with us on the way?" (Luke 24:32). But these hearts walk with him and remain cold; how is it that they remain cold?

The natural body of our Lord, the body born of Mary, is given to us in the Holy Eucharist to be, among other things, the bond of fellowship which unites us as members of his mystical body, the Church. And when some unhappy soul forsakes that fellowship, the doctrine of the Holy Eucharist, because it is so dear, because it is so central to us, is commonly the first doctrine which it learns to disown, and to blaspheme. Let us, then, gathered in the Church of the Blessed Sacrament, on the feast of the Holy Sacrament, in the presence of the Blessed Sacrament, offer reparation to our divine Lord for the treachery of those unworthy followers of his, in England and in all parts of the world, who have gone back and walk no more with him; let us offer reparation especially for the insults with which these his rebellious children assail him, in the Sacrament of the altar. And, while we do that, let us offer reparation too for the little love which is shown him even by the souls that have not forsaken him; for the little love we ourselves show him, when we receive him so coldly, so indevoutly, in our own communions. He asks us, from his throne in the monstrance, whether we too will go away. Let us resolve, by his grace, to draw all the nearer to him, to walk all the closer at his side, worshipping not less devoutly with the four thousand than with the five thousand. For he has the words of eternal life, without which man must remain for ever disconsolate, and the world waste itself, over shadows, lost in its wilderness.

XXVIII

The Hidden God

Verily thou art a God that hidest thyself. (Isa. 45:15)

GOD HIDES HIMSELF IN HIS CREATION. That sounds an extraordinary thing to say; for it is in his creation that God reveals himself. The works of his hands manifest him to us, as the unoriginated cause without which they had never been; as the uncommunicated impulse which kindles their sluggish pulses into life; as the necessary being which underprops the caducity of their paste-board existence; as the supreme perfection which their varying degrees of excellence imply, by approximating to it; as the mind which marshals them in that deliberate order which our minds find there, but cannot put there. Yet, so revealing himself to those who patiently seek for him, from those who indolently ignore the message he conceals himself. Our first parents, when they had sinned, hid from God's face amidst the trees of the garden, took refuge in the creature to find an escape from the Creator. And to this day the soul that is chained to earth by selfishness or frivolity loses itself in creatures, cannot look above them or beyond them because it will not. Man has the fatal power of not thinking. So God allows himself to be blasphemed by those who deny his existence; he, whose very essence is to exist. From millions of mankind he hides the very principle of his nature.

Sacrament Most Holy

God hides himself in his government of the world, in the process of history. The Jews knew that; their bewilderment over it runs through the whole of the Old Testament like a plaintive refrain: "Why standest thou so far off, O Lord, and hidest thy face in the needful time of trouble?" (Ps. 10:1). Dominated as they were by the notion of strict justice, of an exact proportion between sin and suffering as punishment for sin, they were baffled by the spectacle of a world in which they, God's chosen people, were condemned to defeat and to captivity, while the bloodthirsty heathen flourished. And we too, after all these centuries, are not exempt from the same misgivings. Have not we seen Catholic nations go under in the struggle for survival; laborious edifices of Catholic life and culture demolished at a blow? Or, if we turn to individual lives whose history is known to us, do we find the most devoted and unselfish characters of our acquaintance rewarded, in this world, with prosperity? Do we find that scheming wickedness always defeats its own ends? In our own lives, less obscure to us in the hidden springs of their conduct, can we pretend that it is always our most earnest prayers which have been answered, always the actions that were performed with the purest motives that have brought us happiness? We know that it is not so; God will not make the riddle of existence as easy for us as that. He hides himself; bids his sun shine upon the evil and the good; sends rain upon the just and the unjust (Matt. 5:45).

The time came, in God's mercy, when he would make a fuller revelation of himself to man. Now at last, we thought, all would be plain; there can be no more concealment, when God himself comes down to live amongst his creatures. Under whatever conditions he takes human nature upon himself, conscious divinity cannot but shine through. If we thought that, we were doomed to disappointment. He came, and the world missed the portents of his coming. The stars could not keep the secret, they blurted it out to the wise men, their cronies; the angels could not keep the secret, they sang it to the shepherds over the fields of Bethlehem. But the world, the world of fashion and intelligence, was looking the other way. What, after all, was there for it to see? A baby, crying at its mother's breast; a boy working in a carpenter's shop; a street-corner orator, producing a nine-days' wonder among the fisher-folk at Capharnaum; a discredited popular leader, ignominiously put to death; a corpse lying in a tomb—and this was God! He rose again, but in doing so he showed himself to none but a handful of chosen witnesses; the world looked to find him, and he was gone. Would you know that Jesus Christ is divine? Then see how he imitates, in his humanity, the reticence of the God who created the world and left it to forget him, the God who rules the world, yet rules it imperceptibly; and recognize, in the masterpiece of his Incarnation, the touch of the same artist's brush.

The hidden God, whom so many have looked for and have not found; the hidden God, whose presence, even in our best times of prayer, is so fugitive, that we reach only the ante-chamber which he, the Master of the house, has just left—did we think, that when he came to live on earth afresh in his greatest sacrament it would be easy for us to discover him? No, in the Holy Eucharist he repeats and surpasses the mystery in which all our knowledge of his being is involved. No longer content to hide *behind* his creation, he hides *in* his creation. He conceals from us, this time, not merely the

Sacrament Most Holy

principle on which his favours are distributed, but the very knowledge whether his favours have been bestowed or not. And he gives himself afresh into the hands of men, not with the obedience of a human will but, if we may dare to say so, with the mechanical compliance which we expect of material things—gives himself, not merely as a servant but as an instrument, to be used by us and for us. Let me draw that out a little more in detail.

God hides himself in his creation, in the sense that you cannot read in it the evidence to prove his existence unless you will use your reason to do so. If you will use it, reason points to God as surely as the compass to the magnetic pole. But where he hides himself in the Holy Eucharist, reason gives us no indication at all. It can tell us, what the senses cannot tell us, that there is an underlying reality which sustains, in natural objects, those outward appearances which impress themselves on our senses. But, that when the priest has spoken the words of consecration that underlying reality is withdrawn from the appearances of bread and wine, that the reality of Christ's body and blood becomes present instead—over all that reason has no message to give us; nothing, here, will point to God's presence except the divining-wand of faith. Here, then, more than ever, he exposes himself to the mocking incredulity of the profane.

God hides himself in his government of the world, in the sense that he does not, ordinarily, allow us to see which are his chosen friends by singling them out for his special favours. But he does show us, by common experience, what harm can flow from the misuse of his creatures, when we indulge in them wrongly. In the Holy Eucharist, he does not do even that. We know that the Holy

RONALD KNOX

Eucharist is a sun which fosters supernatural life in those who receive it worthily, rain which gives them growth; is a sun which dries up life in the soul which receives it unworthily, rain which brings with it only corruption. But all this is hidden from our eyes; you cannot tell whether the gift brought death or life to the communicant who knelt next to you this morning. In his operation, as in his presence, God hides himself here more effectively than ever.

And if, in his Incarnation, God stooped towards us and condescended to our level by uniting his divine nature with a human nature, which, though created, was yet created in his own image, possessing intellect and will, how much lower he stoops, how much more he condescends, when he hides himself in the Holy Eucharist, veiled under the forms of material, insensible things! If in his Incarnation he gave himself up into the hands of men, allowed them to overpower and control his movements, how much more generously does he give himself in the Holy Eucharist, putting himself into the priest's hands and exposing himself to outrage from his enemies! In food and drink, dumb ministers of our human satisfaction, he finds the most secure hiding-place of all.

If, then, this secrecy is characteristic of God's dealings with us, what account, what explanation are we to give of it? Two purposes, at least, it manifestly fulfils. It demands of us an exercise of faith; and it inspires us with an example of resignation.

An exercise of faith—we are apt to be a little impatient when we are told that; just as we are a little impatient when we are told that hard work is good for us because it braces the mind, or that suffering has a purpose because it softens the heart. But that is because we do not understand what faith means. We think of it as a kind

Sacrament Most Holy

of second-best, a substitute, a jury-mast, with which we have to be content when reason fails us. But faith, if you come to think of it, is something very much more than that. Considered as an intellectual process, it is inferior to reason, because it gives us no better than a dim and reflected light. But if you consider it as a gift infused by God, it is something higher than reason, because it breathes the air of a supernatural world which lies beyond all our experience. Your lamp may be brighter than the uncertain glimmerings of dawn; but those glimmerings are the foretaste, the reflected brightness of the daylight which is to come. So faith, less luminous to our minds than reason, is the foretaste of that fuller knowledge which we shall enjoy, please God, in heaven. And faith lives on mystery; that is its proper food; without mystery it can only languish. All those candles, then, in the sanctuary, all that gleam of polished metal, shed upon the sacred Host not light, but darkness; the more they make its outward appearance visible, the more they conceal its inner reality. In that darkness our faith moves, and grasps and welcomes its opportunity.

And this hidden God who challenges our faith teaches us at the same time, by his example, to obliterate ourselves, to annihilate ourselves, as he, so far as may be possible, obliterates himself, annihilates himself here. He gives himself, unresisting, into our hands; we are to give ourselves unresisting into his hands, without struggle, without reservations, without misgiving. "You are dead," St Paul says, "and your life is hidden with Christ in God" (Col. 3:3); the inner reality of our souls is to be something different from anything the world sees; behind the mask of our daily cares and preoccupations there is to be some other foundation for our

RONALD KNOX

lives, a continual aspiration towards God and desire for his presence. And this aspiration of ours is to transform and divinize us; "I live," St Paul says again, "yet now not I, but Christ liveth in me" (Gal. 2:20). As in the Holy Eucharist the body and blood of Christ replace, sacramentally, the substance of the bread and wine, so in our lives, mystically, God's indwelling presence is to replace and supersede the self in us, which is always striving with him for the mastery; we are to be Christ-bearers, vehicles of Christ, nothing more. And just as his presence in the Eucharist is such, that when the sacred species are moved or broken Christ himself is not moved or broken, so this inner life of ours is to make us indifferent to all the outward happenings which affect our earthly fortunes; good or evil chance will affect only the outer fringes of our experience, not ourselves. We shall be hidden men, as befits those who do service to the hidden God.

God hides himself; it is by that sign that we are to recognize him. Look up, then, Christian hearts, and see God enthroned in the monstrance; for here, hidden more than anywhere else, more than anywhere else he is revealed.

XXIX

The Mirror of Conscience

It is given to us, all alike, to catch the glory of the Lord as in a mirror, and so we become transfigured into the same likeness. (2 Cor. 3:18)

THERE IS ONE MOMENT during the Mass, just about the *Domine non sum dignus*, when the priest, if he is not careful, catches sight of his own features reflected in the paten, as he bends down over it. I've always felt that this rather unwelcome experience had the makings of a sermon in it.

You see, at that moment the priest has no eyes except for the sacred Host. The management of his eyes, all through the Mass, is carefully prescribed by rubric, in such a way as to guard him from distraction. Roughly speaking, you may say that they should be focused, all the time, on one or other of these things, the book, the cross above the altar, the sacred elements, and the floor. And if the priest keeps to that principle, he almost forgets the rest of his surroundings, except in so far as the banging and bashing and coughing and dropping of pennies in the background keeps him reminded of them. Then, just at that sacred moment, an alien thing intrudes upon his thoughts, the sight of his own features. At the

---

This sermon was preached to convent school girls.

same time, it is the kind of distraction he can make good use of. Because he will do well to consider the contrast between what he sees on the paten, and what he meant (and was meant) to see there. He looked there to catch sight of a sinless Victim; he caught sight, instead, of a sinful priest. *Domine, non sum dignus*—how can *this* be worthy to receive *that*?

And now, let me suggest that the sacred Host, in its own way, is a mirror; is a kind of supernatural looking-glass which (as is the way with supernatural things) does just the opposite of what we should expect it to do. You sometimes look in the looking-glass, don't you? It's not a habit I want to encourage; it's a painful exercise for some of us, and a dangerous exercise for others. But, from time to time, the state of our hair or one thing and another makes it necessary that we should. Now, what is it that you see? You see another girl doing her hair, and finding out how to do it by looking at you. And the odd thing is this, that you have complete control over that other girl's movements; you can impose your will on her. If you make a face, she has to make the same face; if you dodge to one side, she has to dodge to one side; if you scratch your nose, she has to scratch her nose, too. And you are exactly alike, except for one rather important point of difference. Put it in this way if your father or mother turned up while you were doing your hair, and the nuns asked, "Which of these two girls would you rather have sent home for the holidays?" there would be no difficulty about the answer. The answer would be, "I'd rather have this one, if you don't mind, because this one's real. The other one looks just the same, but she wouldn't do as well, because she isn't real." That's the point about your reflection; it's got everything you've got except reality.

Sacrament Most Holy

Now, if you come to think of it, with the Blessed Sacrament it is just the other way round; it is just the opposite of a reflection in the looking-glass. Our Lord saw his own image sometimes. He saw it in our Lady's eyes, when he looked up at them from his cradle. He saw it in the waters of Jordan, when he went down into them to be baptized. He saw it miraculously reflected in St Veronica's handkerchief, on the way to his crucifixion. But what he saw then wasn't real. It looked like himself, but it wasn't himself. It was just the other way when he stood by the table at the Last Supper, and said, "This is my body." His eyes were fixed on something that didn't look like himself but *was* himself. It looked like an ordinary piece of bread; but the reality wasn't just a piece of bread. The reality was something more real than that. It was himself, who is reality. What looked like a piece of bread was, you see, a kind of supernatural mirror—not reflecting, as other mirrors do, the appearance without the reality; it reflected the reality without the appearance.

That, then, is what you see when the priest lifts his hands over his head at the time of the Consecration. You see a supernatural mirror, which, instead of presenting the appearance of our Lord to your eyes, presents the reality of our Lord to your mind. And you mustn't be stupid about it, and say, "I wish he would present the reality to my eyes; then I should find it so much easier to think about him at Mass." Because the reality is something which can't be presented to your eyes, it can only be represented to your mind. When you see your face in the glass, you see something which is less real than it looks. When you see the sacred Host, you see something which is more real than it looks. That's the difference.

It would be easy to point out other ways in which the Blessed

RONALD KNOX

Sacrament reminds us of a mirror. There's this for instance—suppose you break a looking-glass. I hope you won't, because they say it is an unlucky thing to do, and I'm sure the nuns would make you feel that you had done something unlucky if you did. But if you break a looking-glass, that other girl hasn't disappeared; on the contrary, she has multiplied. Look in any of the broken pieces, and that other girl is still there. At least, she isn't there really, because there never was any other girl really; but the whole appearance has reproduced itself in each broken piece, though it remains just as unreal as before. Now, suppose that the priest is afraid, at communion time, that there won't be enough Hosts to go round; what does he do? He breaks each Host in two. And if you receive half a Host, what do you receive? Half Christ? No, the whole of Christ. The reality has reproduced itself in each broken fragment, the whole reality, and it remains real as ever.

But there's another way in which the Blessed Sacrament can remind us of a mirror, which is more important to what I'm suggesting this afternoon. I was saying, if you remember, that when you look in the looking-glass, what you see there is something which you can influence; it moves when you move, smiles when you smile, looks grave when you look grave—in a word, it models itself on you. When you look at the sacred Host, it is just the other way round. What you see there is not something which you can influence; it is something which can influence you. You've often been told, I expect, what a striking difference there is between the ordinary food you eat, and that heavenly food which is given you in the Blessed Sacrament. When you eat ordinary food, you turn it into yourself. When you eat the body of Christ, he turns you into

Sacrament Most Holy

himself. And in the same way, this mirror of the Blessed Sacrament works in the opposite way from the ordinary mirror. It is not for you to dictate to Jesus Christ what he is to do: you are to let him dictate to you. He is not to model himself on you, you are to model yourself on him. When you look at Jesus in the Blessed Sacrament, say to him: Dear Jesus, I want to imitate you in the same way as my reflection in the looking-glass imitates me. I want to imitate you promptly, and exactly, and persistently, just as my reflection in the looking-glass imitates me.

Imitating Jesus Christ—that's an easy thing to say, but perhaps you complain that it's rather a vague kind of ambition. Well, let's get closer to the idea of the thing. Let's have a look, alternately, at two different mirrors; the mirror of the Blessed Sacrament, which reflects the life Jesus Christ lived on earth, and the mirror of conscience, which reflects (perhaps rather more mistily than it ought to) the life which you and I are living. First of all, let's concentrate on the point I've been making already—that the Blessed Sacrament is something which conceals the reality it contains, which *looks* much less important than it really is. You see, in that respect, it's a perfect mirror of our Lord's own earthly life. All the time, remember, our Lord was concealing his own Godhead, going about the world looking like an ordinary man, talking like an ordinary man, and, what is more, a poor working man; he was born in a stable, and brought up in a carpenter's shop. He would have nothing to do with rank or privilege. And then, when he began to show that his powers were something more than human, look how he kept on trying to hush it up! He cast out the devils, and then enjoined them not to tell anyone about it; he did the same with some of his most remarkable cures; "Go thy way, and tell no man." And his best friends were the apostles, who were, in those days, rather stupid people; they didn't in the least appreciate him. His own relations thought he was mad, and tried to put him under restraint. And even when he was crucified, he wasn't crucified alone, with all the dignity of martyrdom. No, he would have a thief on each side, so that the careless passer-by who didn't bother to read the title on the cross would say, "Another of those thieves, I suppose." Could anything be more unobtrusive than the way in which God went about the world as man?

Yes, and now let's take a look at the mirror of conscience. Do we go about the world always trying to make as little of ourselves as possible? Are we quite indifferent, whether the world at large thinks us important people or not? Do we say to ourselves, "After all, what does it matter?" when our friends don't seem to appreciate us? Do we try to hide away our good qualities, our kind actions—don't we sometimes rather try to draw attention to them? Do we allow ourselves to be misjudged—don't we even, sometimes, try to put a better colour on our own record than it really deserves? Aren't we ashamed of being seen in the company of people whom we regard as inferior to ourselves? One sometimes hears it said of a person, "He's so completely careless of appearances"; if you come to think of it, there's nobody that could be said of with more truth than our blessed Lord. So careless of appearances while he lived on earth, and now, when he comes to us in the Blessed Sacrament, coming to us under appearances of bread and wine—he doesn't mind about appearances, you see, as long as the reality is there. And we—how often, with us, it is just the other way!

Sacrament Most Holy

And then, remember what we were saying about the whole of Christ being present in each particle, when the Host is divided. That, you see, is our Lord's great impartiality; he will give himself alike to each. Our Lord never liked the idea of favouritism. Even when he was told that his blessed Mother and his brethren wanted to see him, he replied in that strange phrase: "Whosoever doeth the will of my Father that is in heaven, he is my brother and sister and mother." And when Salome wanted to secure the two best places in his kingdom for her sons, James and John, he would do nothing about it; "to sit on my right hand and my left is not mine to give" (Matt. 20:26). He is for everybody; he will be the same for everybody, if only they will come to him. Your Host at Mass is just like everybody's else's Host, and it contains the same tremendous reality which everybody else's Host contains. The beggar, when he goes to communion, is on a level with the prince. And now, refer to the mirror of conscience again, and see if we haven't something to learn from our Lord here, something to learn from the Blessed Sacrament here. How difficult it is, not to favouritize; not to treat the people we like with a little more kindness than the people we don't like; to make rather more allowance for their failings, pay rather more attention to their interests! With most of us, there's room here for imitating our Lord more than we do.

And then, there's this to be considered; although our Lord is really present in the Holy Eucharist, he is present in such a way that he cannot be exposed to physical injury. If, for example, by some unfortunate piece of carelessness, the Hosts in the tabernacle were left too long and allowed to corrupt, our Lord's presence, we know, would be withdrawn from them. And that, I think, is a parable of his whole life on earth; living so close to men, and yet so detached from earthly needs. He needs food, yes, but he will not be in any hurry about it, "My meat is to do the will of him who sent me" (John 4:34). He is on board a vessel in imminent danger of shipwreck, and he lies down to sleep (Matt. 8:24). And he is always free to go where he is wanted; "I will come and heal him" (Luke 7:25). "Let us go into Judaea again"—he makes up his mind on the spur of the moment, has no plans. This detachment of his from worldly comforts, from the routine of habit, is a thing we all need, and most of us haven't got it. We all need it, and perhaps especially in these days, when the future of everything is so uncertain. It may easily happen to any of you, that she will find herself, when she grows up, much poorer than she expected to be, that the career she was working for is, for some reason, denied her, that the circumstances of her life will be much more uncomfortable, much more unsettled, than she ever guessed they would be. And that will turn you into a discontented and disillusioned person, unless you can get our Lord to give you that spirit of detachment which was his.

Lord, I am not worthy—I am so full of shams and pretences. Speak the word only, and my soul shall be healed; I shall learn to be more careless of appearances. Lord, I am not worthy—I am so blinded by fondness and prejudice. Speak the word only, and I shall know how to give my best to everybody, as you did, as you do. Lord, I am not worthy—I am so tied to earthly comforts, to worldly plans. Speak the word only, and I shall learn to be detached, as you were, as you are, from all the things of sense.

XXX

Bread from Heaven

Labour not for the meat which perisheth, but for that meat which endureth unto everlasting life. (JOHN 6:27)

IT IS A CURIOUS POINT about our Lord's teaching, or about that part of it at any rate which has been preserved for us by St John, that he is always treating the things of earth, the material things of sense which are familiar to us, as unreal, as mere shadows and appearances, while the true realities, of which these earthly things are but copies, are in heaven. It is our habit to think the other way; to assume that our own flesh and blood, our food and drink and all the comforts we enjoy, are solid realities; heaven is something distant and shadowy—we believe that we shall be happy if we attain to it, but we cannot imagine how, because it all seems so remote from this real world of our experience. We could understand it easily enough if our Lord said, "You see the water in that well? Divine grace is something like that, has the same clearness, the same refreshing qualities, the same power of diffusing itself, that water has." But he doesn't say that; when he talks to the woman of Samaria, he says, "If thou knewest the gift of God, and who it is that saith to thee, Give me to drink, thou wouldst perhaps have asked of him, and he would have given thee living water" (John 4:10).

RONALD KNOX

Living water. This water in Jacob's well, which people come so far to fetch, is only dead water after all; the real water, the living water, is the grace of God from heaven. And the purest water in the world, he seems to tell us, is only a shadow, an inferior copy, of the living stream which flows through the city of God. Always, to him, it is the earthly things that are shams, the heavenly things that are the realities. It is as if he could not accustom himself, in spite of that perfect humanity which he took upon himself at the Incarnation, to look upon things from our human point of view. Grace does not remind him of a draught of water; a draught of water reminds him of grace.

So it is when he refers to himself as the true vine (John 15). He doesn't point to the vine, and tell us that the closeness of union which binds him to us and ourselves to him is something like the closeness of union which binds the vine to its branches, and its branches to the vine. No, he looks at it the other way round. You see that vine? he says. That is not a real vine. All the vines you may see spreading down like a curtain over some hillside in France—they are not real vines, they are only shams, copies of a reality which exists somewhere else. And that reality is his mystical body, the Church. We shall never understand the mystery of organic growth, of that inner principle which bids the same tree put forth, year after year, fruits of its own kind, until we get to heaven and experience, with our Lady and the saints, the reality of that union which binds us to him, that unction which flows from him to us. And we shall never understand the mystery of water, the secret of its pervasive passage through the earth, of its welling up to reach its own level, of its necessity to animal life, until we get to heaven and know what grace means, how, all our lives through, it has been following us and intertwining itself with the experience of daily life, and achieving its work in us, and satisfying the needs of our souls. When we know what the Church is, we shall begin to understand the vine; when we know what grace is, we shall begin to understand water. It is only in heaven that we shall appreciate those satisfying realities, of which we perceive the echoes and the shadows here on earth.

And so it is above all with this great chapter of St John, the sixth chapter, in which, after the miracle of the five thousand, our Lord talks to his disciples about the manna which was sent to the Israelites in the wilderness. "Thou didst give them bread from heaven" (Ps. 77:24; 104:40). the Psalmist wrote, thinking of that wonderful morning in the desert when the hosts of Israel awoke from sleep to find the earth around them white, as with dew, with the strange food that was to be the strengthening of their pilgrimage. But that wasn't really bread from heaven, our Lord says; not the true bread from heaven. And even your experience just now, he implies, when the five loaves were miraculously multiplied so as to satisfy five thousand hungry men—that was not real bread I gave you, not the true bread. I am the bread of life. I am the living bread which came down from heaven. My flesh is real meat; my blood is really drink. All the most palatable food which can tempt your earthly appetites is only a sham, a shadow, a copy of the true bread, mysteriously to be communicated to my faithful followers, which is myself. And once again, not till we reach heaven and understand there what it was that the sacrament of Holy Eucharist has been doing for us all the time, building up our spiritual strength and satisfying our spiritual needs, shall we begin to understand that ordinary process, so familiar in common life, by which the food we eat builds up and strengthens our material bodies.

Let me put it this way, so as to make my point clear. We think of God, don't we, as first of all designing bread for our use, and then, when he came to earth, instituting the Blessed Sacrament under the form of bread so as to remind us of our earthly food? But that wasn't really how it happened. Before he made the world, almighty God foresaw the need for the Incarnation, and decreed the institution of the Holy Eucharist for the benefit of our souls. And he gave us bread, the common bread we eat, to prepare the way for the Holy Eucharist, to be like the Holy Eucharist, to remind us of the Holy Eucharist when it came. Whenever we eat bread, if we really want to see things as they are, we ought to be reminded of the Blessed Sacrament.

A world of shadows, a world of shams—how difficult it would have been to preach that doctrine, in England, forty or fifty years ago! When we supplied the whole world from our factories, and took toll of it twice over, by exporting what we had manufactured! When colonies, newly opened up, seemed to hold out unlimited prospect of riches to the adventurous; when income tax was less than a shilling in the pound, when railway shares seemed like a gold-mine; when British credit seemed a thing as immovable as the laws of nature, and British influence feared no jealousy abroad, no disaffection in the Dominions. Look about you, as you pass through once prosperous suburbs, or peep between the railings of the parks that fringe our country roads, and see the great houses men built for themselves in those days, with the secure confidence of handing them down to a grateful posterity. Oh, there was poverty, there was misery; but all that was being taken in hand, was to be eliminated almost at once; universal education and a little town-planning would put an end to that. How peaceful they were, those grandfathers of ours, in their possessions; how eagerly they pulled down their barns to build greater, and told themselves that they had much substance laid up for many years!

"We don't want to fight, but by jingo if we do—we've got the ships, we've got the men, we've got the money, too"[1]; so ran our popular sentiment in 1878, only a little over fifty years ago.

And now? "Your fathers," our Lord says to the Jews, "did eat manna, and are dead." More highly privileged than any other nation on earth, they found their daily needs supplied without any effort on their part; they had only to look round them and to gather in their daily bread, the bread of angels. And yet, it was only their earthly needs that bread supplied. In the course of time they died, and their bones lay white in the wilderness, white as the manna which fell around their tents while they still had need of it. Might he not say to us, too, "Your fathers did eat manna"? He gave them abundance of material riches; they were the envy of the world. And now they are dead, and they have not even left to us their prosperity, the comfortable certainties which they enjoyed in life. We, their descendants, find our legislators hurrying to and fro—and in the shooting season—to balance the budget, to save the pound. The pound sterling, which used to be as solid a fact as the sun in the sky, had to be saved! And we look about us nervously, wondering what is going to be taxed next, whose salary is going to be cut next. Nor is

---

1. G. W. Hunt, "We Don't Want to Fight" (music-hall song).

it ourselves only that have felt the pinch; Australia has had its crisis, Germany has had its crisis, the United States have their unemployment problem, far worse than ours. And we look at the houses our grandfathers built, now advertised hopelessly for sale, or left untenanted because their owners cannot afford to live in them, and ask ourselves what has happened.

And what has happened? Has there been a great drought, a wholesale destruction of crops by flood or by blight? Why no, there is more food in the world than we know what to do with. "Thou hast put gladness in my heart," says the Psalmist, "since their corn and wine and oil increased" (Ps. 4:7–8). But when our corn and wine and oil increase, it gives us no gladness; we burn the unwanted stocks of grain, we block up the oil-wells, for fear of over-production. What has happened? Nothing that we can see, nothing that we can blame. Our own laws of supply and demand, based on the desire of every man to get as rich as he can as quick as he can, have caught us in their toils; we are the prisoners of our own machine, and we cannot get out of it. Tell me, did we not do well to say that this is an unreal world we live in? A world in which mere abstractions, like the laws of supply and demand, can bring men to the verge of starvation, when there is food ready for them to eat, being burned because no price can be got for it?

If thou knewest the gift of God! If we could only see the realities of the other world as they! God grant that this glimpse he has just given us of the hollowness and unreality of our own may enlighten us a little, may make us begin to understand how much it is we miss when we neglect the sacraments, or treat them carelessly and approach them without preparation and without reverence. That

Sacrament Most Holy

heavenly dole, proportioned to the needs of each, freely given, and despised by its recipients, God help us all, because it is given freely. Remember, it is very easy for us, in critical times like these, to become all the more attached to worldly advantages and to material comforts, because we see them ready to slip between our fingers; to plunge ourselves feverishly into the enjoyment of the moment, in the hope of shaking off the black load of care that lurks at the back of our minds. But that is not the lesson God means us to read in our present distress. He means us to draw all the closer to him, as the worldly prosperity that made us forget him is taken away from us; to throw ourselves all the more lovingly into his arms, as we see our prospects more uncertain, and our labours less profitable. *Come to me, all you that labour and are burdened*; it was not to one age, or to the inhabitants of one country, that that loving invitation was issued. He calls us away from a world of shadows into a world of realities; from the perplexities of our earthly citizenship to a city which has foundations whose builder and maker is God.

XXXI

The Divine Sacrifice

I live, now not I, but Christ liveth in me. (GAL. 2:20)

TODAY A SPECIAL CIRCUMSTANCE marks out our observance of the Corpus Christi festival. The priest who is singing the Mass is singing Mass for the first time, fresh from his ordination on Sunday. And it is an instinct among faithful Christians—not a rule, prescribed by authority, not a doctrine set down in text-books, but one of those instincts which bloom self-sown, from the soil of Christian piety—that we should make much of a newly-ordained priest; kiss his hands while the oil still glistens on them, obtain his blessing before that ceremony is staled by usage. A virtue and an influence must hang, we feel, about the first sacerdotal acts which the neophyte performs. We can quote Gospel precedent; our Lord would be born of a virgin, he would be buried in a tomb wherein man was never yet laid, and when he rode into Jerusalem before his Passion, the beast that carried him should be a beast no man had ever ridden before; and does not he too delight in the fresh fervour of a priest newly ordained! Does not he pardon us if, for once, our thoughts stray from the sacrifice to him who offers it! Today, then, because the whole institution of the priesthood is so closely bound up with the Mass and with the Eucharist, I do not hesitate to make

Sacrament Most Holy

the institution of the priesthood my subject. Today's feast, after all, is but the echo of Maundy Thursday—Maundy Thursday, with all its sorrow turned into gladness. And what our Lord did at the Last Supper, he accompanied with the words, "Do this"; it was not only the first Mass but the first ordination.

When God created sun and moon and stars, and the earth with all its delicate beauty, its intricate workmanship, he pronounced it very good; and the sons of God shouted for joy at the birth of this new creation. But within the material universe itself there was no answering cry of recognition. True, the stars in their courses, the mysterious alternation of light and darkness, the orderly process of the seasons, showed forth the glory of him who ordained them; true, the living things could enjoy some confused pleasures of memory and of hope, and in doing so rendered continually a kind of unconscious praise to their Creator. But amid all that wealth of multitudinous life there was no conscious response given, no reasonable homage. So God took of the slime of the earth, and made man; breathed into his nostrils the breath of life, and man became a living soul. Man was to be the priest of creation, was to praise God on behalf of those mute, material things, with a mind that could reason and a voice to express its reasonings. The priest of creation; the instrument through which the chorus of its gratitude should thrill and become vocal at last.

Centuries later, we have no means of knowing how many centuries later, God breathed into the face of man once more. "When he had said this, he breathed on them, and said, Receive ye the Holy Ghost" (John 20:22). When he had rested on the seventh day after the stupendous achievement of the natural creation, God made man to be its priest. When he rose on the third day after resting from the labours of his Passion, Incarnate God set the crown on his work of redemption by instituting the Christian priesthood. It was a fresh act of creation, no less amazing in its results than that other; for the powers which the Christian priesthood enjoys exceed the natural powers of man no less significantly than man's natural powers exceed those of the brute beasts. The world, fallen and redeemed, was to be reconciled to God by the ministry of the priest—a representative man, chosen out among his fellows to be their spokesman and God's ambassador. Sanctified by his office, he was to intercede for his sinful brethren, to come between them and God's anger, offering sacrifice in their name.

True, there was nothing unheard of in that. For centuries before our Lord came priests had been offering sacrifice to God; among the Jews, in obedience to the light of an imperfect revelation, among the Gentiles, from a sort of blind instinct which warned them that atonement for sin, could it only be achieved, was the first step towards communion with God. But all those old sacrifices were no better than a frantic appeal, a despairing gesture. The blood of bulls and goats could not take away sin (Heb. 10:4); and the priests who offered them were themselves encompassed with infirmities; sinful men themselves, they could not bear the petitions of the people into God's presence as having the right to enter it. Our Lord came, to be at once a sinless Victim and a sinless Priest. Priest and Victim, he offered his own death to be the sufficient atonement for a world's transgressions. When the first Adam received the breath of life, this material universe was elevated into a fresh state of communion with God. When the second Adam gave back that same breath

Sacrament Most Holy

of life into his Father's hands, our guilty race was restored to the divine favour. Ruined long since by Adam's fault, the world could cry once more: *Habemus Pontificem.*

It would have been possible, it might even have seemed natural, that our Lord, when he achieved our redemption, should apply thenceforward the virtue and the effects of that redemption to human souls without any kind of priestly ministry to aid his purpose. Many who value the name of Christian still find it reasonable to believe that he did so; the priesthood, they will tell you, was an institution which belonged to a former age of imperfect revelation; when the mercy of God shone out to us in the face of Jesus Christ, the need for all ceremonies and sacraments was done away. But it is not so that the courtesy of our Lord Jesus Christ treats us. When he turned water into wine at Cana of Galilee, he used no word, no touch, no gesture, to claim the miracle as his own. "Fill the water-pots with water.... Draw out now, and bear it to the governor of the feast" (John 2:8)—the miraculous transformation should take its effect between the hands of the servants who were ministering to the guests; they should have the apparent credit for it. And so it was when he multiplied the loaves in the wilderness. He gave the loaves and fishes to the disciples to distribute; it was in their hands, it seems, that the multiplication took place. It is part of his courtesy that he should thus associate human agents with himself, then when most he manifests his superhuman powers. Their obedience to his command shall be the immediate occasion of those prodigies whose operation, in the last resort, can only come from him.

So it is, then, with his new priesthood. Not only when he gives us, under the forms of bread and wine, his own body and blood to be our food; in all the sacraments he is the true author, the true fountain of grace, yet he will suffer a human ministry to intervene—"Receive ye the Holy Ghost; whose sins ye shall remit, they are remitted unto them, and whose sins ye shall retain they are retained" (John 20:22). But most, and most characteristically, in the sacrament of Holy Eucharist. When a priest baptizes or absolves, he stands there, sits there, only to unseal the fountains of grace in answer to the faith and penitence which knock to receive them. But when he stands at the altar the priest does something more; he takes upon himself the person of Christ, re-enacting in his name the ceremony which he performed on the night before his Passion. A priest clad in the sacred vestments (says the author of the *Imitation*) is the vice-regent of Christ himself.[1] He uses our Lord's own words, identifies himself with the offering which our Lord continually makes before the Father of his own body and blood. How is it that men can be found with the assurance, with the presumption, to do that?

The difficulty is solved for us by one golden phrase of St John Chrysostom's. "When you see a priest offering the sacrifice," he says, "do not think as if it were *he* that is doing this; it is the hand of Christ, invisibly stretched forth." The hand of Christ invisibly stretched forth—that is the image we must conjure up if we are to think of the Mass as what it really is. The philosopher Aristotle, in defining the position of a slave, uses the words, "A slave is a living tool." And that is what a priest is, a living tool of Jesus Christ. He lends his hands to be Christ's hands, his voice to be Christ's voice,

---

1. *Imitation of Christ*, Book IV, ch. 5.

Sacrament Most Holy

his thoughts to be Christ's thoughts; there is, there should be, nothing of himself in it from first to last, except where the Church graciously permits him to dwell for a moment in silence on his own special intentions, for the good estate of the living and the dead. Those who are not of our religion are puzzled sometimes, or even scandalized, by witnessing the ceremonies of the Mass; it is all, they say, so mechanical. But you see, it *ought* to be mechanical. They are watching, not a man, but a living tool; it turns this way and that, bends, straightens itself, gesticulates, all in obedience to a preconceived order—Christ's order, not ours. The Mass is best said—we Catholics know it—when it is said so that you do not notice how it is said; we do not expect eccentricities from a tool, the tool of Christ.

That notion is not a mere fancy; the Church herself is at pains to emphasize it in the ordination rite. If you have witnessed the ceremonies of an ordination, you will have seen the ordination candidates stretched out at their full length face downwards, like corpses, like dummies, while the solemn chant of the litany rolls over their heads. They are waiting there like dead things, for the Holy Spirit to come and quicken them into a new form of life; as Adam's body waited, slime of the earth, for the informing touch of the Creator's hand to quicken him into a living soul. They are yielding their bodies to Christ to be his instruments, as completely as if they had no life, no volition of their own. And even when they have risen from the ground, you will see their hands being tied together with purificators, in token that they are the captives of Jesus Christ, his slaves, to drive and control as he wills. "I live, now not I, but Christ liveth in me"—that is the protestation which these ceremonies make on behalf of the newly-ordained priest. No life of his own, no liberty of his own; henceforth he is Christ's.

Whenever the holy mysteries are celebrated, Christ is doubly present at the altar; present in the sacrifice, and present in the priest. Still, as in the cenacle, both gift and giver are himself. In the sacrifice, as we know, he is present after a special sacramental manner; the outward forms of bread and wine inhere in, are held together by, an underlying reality which is the very substance of his own body and blood. He is present in the actions of the priest not physically but mystically, taking them into himself and making them his own. "I live, now not I, but Christ liveth in me"; that should be the reflection of every priest every time he goes to the altar; in no other confidence could he dare to use the words he uses, to handle that which he handles. But with that thought comes, or should come, a further reflection—this identification of my voice, my thoughts, my will with Christ, is it meant to take effect only for one short half-hour of the day, when I put on the sacred vestments of my calling? Is it not rather his demand that my will, my intentions, my judgments should be made one with his, not for half an hour of the day but for twenty-four hours? To one who remembers that, vocation to the priesthood is hedged about with no ordinary terrors. Dare we priests believe that Christ lives in us?

Our brethren of the laity often complain of the priests they get; I wonder, does it ever occur to them to pray for better? When the Ember seasons come round, how many people remember to pray for the priests who are being ordained? We pile the sanctuary with flowers, we make it a blaze of candles; but there is something else needed far more than lights or flowers for God's honour, that the

Sacrament Most Holy

hearts of his priests should be made a fit habitation for himself. Of his priests? Not of his priests only, but our own hearts, too. When he comes to us in communion, he comes, not to bring some transient influence, but that he may live, more and more, in us. In the miracle of transubstantiation, the substance of his creatures is really, physically replaced by the substance of his own body. And the effect of the Sacrament in you should conform to the same model; your self, your will, should die more and more, be replaced more and more by himself, by his will; choosing for you, operating in you, sanctifying your thoughts and inspiring your actions, the centre and heart of your being. Today is your patronal feast. If this church were dedicated to some martyr or confessor, I would be urging you to imitate his actions, to be like him. But since this church takes its title from the Blessed Sacrament, I will urge you rather to be like the Blessed Sacrament; to let Christ live in you, to let him make you the abiding dwelling-place of his presence. May he grant that blessing both to priests and people, that his life may grow more and more in them, absorb them more and more into himself; till at last in that heavenly temple where sacrifice and sacrament are done away, we shall see him as he is, and worship him as he ought to be worshipped.